Every Farm Tells a Story

Every Farm
Tells a Story

~

A Tale of Family Farm Values

Jerry Apps

WISCONSIN HISTORICAL SOCIETY PRESS

Published by the Wisconsin Historical Society Press
Publishers since 1855

The Wisconsin Historical Society helps people connect to the past by collecting, preserving, and sharing stories. Founded in 1846, the Society is one of the nation's finest historical institutions. *Join the Wisconsin Historical Society:* wisconsinhistory.org/membership

Printed in the United States of America
Cover: *Near Hartford* by Andy Fletcher. 2017. Oil on canvas. 25" x 40"
Cover design by Sara DeHaan
Typesetting by Shawn Biner

22 21 20 19 18   1 2 3 4 5

Library of Congress Cataloging-in-Publication Data
Names: Apps, Jerry, 1934– author.
Title: Every farm tells a story : a tale of family values / Jerry Apps.
Description: Wisconsin Historical Society Press edition. | Madison : Wisconsin Historical Society Press, 2018. |
Identifiers: LCCN 2017034032 (print) | LCCN 2017053719 (e-book) | ISBN 9780870208645 (E-book) | ISBN 9780870208638 (paperback)
Subjects: LCSH: Farm life—Wisconsin—Wautoma Region—Anecdotes. | Family Farms—Wisconsin—Wautoma Region—Anecdotes. | Apps, Jerold W., 1934– | BISAC: BIOGRAPHY & AUTOBIOGRAPHY / Cultural Heritage. | BIOGRAPHY & AUTOBIOGRAPHY / Personal Memoirs. | LITERARY COLLECTIONS / Essays. | HISTORY / United States / State & Local / Midwest (IA, IL, IN, KS, MI, MN, MO, ND, NE, OH, SD, WI). | HISTORY / United States / 20th Century.
Classification: LCC S521.5.W6 (e-book) | LCC S521.5.W6 A659 2018 (print) | DDC 630.9775/57—dc23
LC record available at https://lccn.loc.gov/2017034032

To my mother, who did so much for our family,
including carefully keeping the account books
on which this book is based.

Contents

Acknowledgments

My brothers, Donald and Darrel, deserve much credit for this book. Before writing the first draft, I spent several hours with them, recalling the stories of our growing-up years on the farm. Later they read the manuscript, corrected me in several places, and added information that I had long forgotten.

My son Steve and my daughter, Susan, read sections of the manuscript and offered many suggestions for improvement. My wife, Ruth, read several drafts of this book, each time offering suggestions and insights on how to make it better.

Danielle J. Ibister, Voyageur Press editor, was of immense help in making this book more readable, as well as more accurate and informative. Her untiring work is most appreciated.

Introduction to the New Edition

Not long after my mother died in 1993, I found the account books she had kept for nearly fifty years, starting when she and my father moved to our home farm in 1924. Although she had but a seventh-grade education, my mother was a meticulous record-keeper, noting every purchase, no matter how small, and every cent of income. I read an entry from 1945: *Farmall H Tractor—$1,750.00* . . . and I remembered when, in the fall of 1945, the first tractor had arrived on our farm and the heavy work of plowing and cultivating became tasks for the tractor. I continued paging through the books, each entry bringing back a flood of memories. And with each memory came more stories to write.

When I finished writing the manuscript for *Every Farm Tells a Story* in 2003 and turned it in to Voyageur Press, the publisher of the first edition, I worried how readers would respond to it. Actually, I wondered if anyone would respond to it at all. This is a book based on simple things: the everyday life of a farm family living and working together during the latter years of the Great Depression and into the 1950s. It's a book about threshing crews and haymaking, about free outdoor movies on Tuesday evenings, about welcoming new neighbors and weeding the pickle patch. But it's also about much more than that. Those of us who grew up on farms in the 1930s to 1950s saw profound changes occur, both on our farms and in our rural communities. We also learned valuable lessons and gained values that most of us have found useful throughout our lives. *Do your chores without complaining. Show up on time. Do every job well. Always try to do better. Never stop learning.*

Every Farm Tells a Story

Next year will be better. Care for others, especially those who have less than you. Accept those who are different from you. Love the land.

When the first edition was released in 2005, I was surprised by the reactions of readers all across the country. A reviewer in Washington state wrote, "*Every Farm Tells a Story* is destined to become the book everyone points to . . . to extol the virtues of rural living . . . fun to read, personal, warm." Another reviewer noted, "As Apps tells it, life was much harder back in those days, before electricity, running water, milking machines, hay balers, combines, corn huskers, and local fire departments. But families and communities worked together and were closer."

Many of the stories in this book are included in the first hour-long television documentary I did, *Jerry Apps: A Farm Story*, which was produced by Wisconsin Public Television in 2012 and was shown on public TV stations across the country. After the show aired I received phone calls, emails, and letters from Maine to California, from Florida to North Dakota, many of them sharing stories similar to mine. Much of what's in this book has touched people far beyond what I ever expected. I'm pleased that the Wisconsin Historical Society Press is bringing *Every Farm Tells a Story* back into print for fans and for a new generation of readers.

Preface

The Account Books

Recently, while rummaging through some boxes I stored after my parents died, I found a set of my mother's meticulously kept farm account books. The records start when my parents moved to the home farm in 1924 and continue until 1973 when they sold the farm and moved to town. Ma wrote in pencil and recorded every penny earned and spent on our central-Wisconsin farm.

I was born in 1934 and, along with my brothers, grew up during the middle years of Ma's record books. My brothers, Donald and Darrel, are twins, born three and a half years after me. In those closing years of the Great Depression and into World War II, our family farmed not too differently from the pioneers who had arrived nearly a hundred years earlier. Horses and humans powered the machines that worked the land. Kerosene lamps and lanterns lighted the house and barn. A windmill pumped water; later, a gasoline engine replaced the less dependable windmill. A one-room country school provided the education for all the area's farm children, ages five to thirteen.

My brothers and I attended the Chain O' Lake School, about one mile south of our farm. Ma had attended the same school when she was a child, and one year I had the same teacher who had taught my mother in the 1910s. Some of the neighborhood kids walked a long way to school. It was about two and a half miles for the Kolka boys at the west end of the school district, and even farther for Mike and Helen Korleski, who lived to the east.

What we didn't realize during those years was that the family farm was changing in profound ways. Some historians claim 1940 to 1955 represents the second great revolution in agriculture; the first occurred hundreds of years earlier when horses and oxen replaced human power.

On our home farm during those years of change, running water allowed cows to drink from individual cups in their stalls instead of one tank in the barnyard. A milking machine, powered by a Briggs & Stratton gasoline engine, sped up the milking process. A factory-produced Farmall H replaced our old homemade tractor that Jim Colligan, the local blacksmith and welder, had converted from a Ford truck. The horses stayed on, albeit in much lesser roles; as Pa said, no matter how cold it was, the horses always started. Most significantly, electric wires were strung to rural farms, and electric lights took over for kerosene lamps and lanterns. Electric motors powered Ma's washing machine and blessedly replaced the milking machine's increasingly temperamental gasoline engine. Hay balers dramatically changed haymaking, while grain combines replaced threshing machines and revolutionized grain harvest.

Ma's farm account books chronicle nearly all of these changes, in one way or another, by way of costs for everything from our first Sears, Roebuck and Co. milking machine to the used telephone pole that supported our first electric yard light.

Now, as I thumb through these account books, the stories return. I include several in these pages, the way I remember living them. The stories are personal and sometimes difficult to tell, since farm life is often not easy or fun-filled. There was a time when I wouldn't tell these stories; in fact, I would have been ashamed to do so. During college, I decided I didn't want anyone to know that I had grown up on a farm without electricity, milked cows by hand, or attended a one-room country school.

I wanted to be viewed as a cosmopolitan young man, an urbane person who knew the ways of the world. I tried to deny my rural upbringing.

After college, I immediately entered the army, where I had lots of time to think. The Korean War had just wound down, and the army contained an excess of fresh second-lieutenants. It occurred to me, during those long months in the military, that I couldn't reject my rural roots. I remember vividly one of my field training exercises in Fort Eustis, Virginia. My unit traveled to Camp A. P. Hill, several miles north of Fort Eustis, and set up camp. We were to conduct mock war exercises, living in two-man pup tents, eating off mess kits, and marching untold miles through thick woods on narrow, vine-covered paths.

My pup-tent partner had grown up in New York City. When the sun went down, he heard danger everywhere. He would wake me in the middle of the night, nearly frantic about some sound he'd heard and how we'd better have our rifles at the ready. No matter that we had no live ammunition.

While he complained about everything in that Virginia woods, I enjoyed the experience immensely. It reminded me of evenings on the farm and the night sounds we country folk took for granted. That experience, and several that followed, helped me see that being a country boy had its advantages, helped me appreciate what others abhorred, and allowed me to function while others—we had several New York boys in our unit—stumbled through the woods, sleep deprived and complaining.

During my time in the army, it occurred to me that who I was, what I believed, what I valued, and how I saw the world were embedded in me so deeply that I often was not even aware of the influences. The beliefs I came to understand at that time are still with me today: I believe that everyone has a responsibility for himself, his family, and his community; humility gives a person dignity; the individual and the community are both sources of great strength; and perseverance and a strong work ethic serve people well, no matter what their life work.

I finally realized that my roots were in the land and no matter what I said, or what I did, I couldn't deny this. Who I am today originates from the home farm, from neighbors, dusty roads, country schools, small towns, and especially the land. The land is a powerful teacher.

The land taught me patience—it produces a crop in its own time, not according to my schedule. The land taught me wonder— the surprise that comes from planting a tiny seed and seeing it grow in one summer into a corn plant seven feet tall. The land taught me respect—to not abuse it by plowing up and down hills, or planting huge fields that the wind can sweep across, causing soil and crops to wash or blow away. And perhaps most importantly, the land taught me to never forget that we are but visitors, temporary stewards, and what we do with the land will dramatically affect those who follow us. Caring for the land is one way to care for the future.

The past fifty years have witnessed phenomenal changes in society. Only a tiny percentage of the population now lives on farms and produces the food and fiber for this nation and beyond. We accept this fact as economic reality. Yet, I believe we should not forget the small family farms that once dotted this country, nor the important contributions they made, not only to feed and clothe the nation but to provide several generations with a set of enduring beliefs and values.

⁓

CHAPTER 1

Family Farm Values

Fork handle—$.65
Mash for chickens—$7.15
One milk pail—$1.15
Horse collar and pad—$8.15
Gloves for Herm—$.52

Chores started on the home farm when you were around four years old, depending on, as Pa would say, "how much meat you have on your bones." The first chore was filling the kitchen and dining room wood boxes. You had to be strong enough to carry an armful of oak wood sticks from the woodshed into the house, and careful enough not to make a mess. Ma didn't like messes, and a stick dropped on her recently swept linoleum floor constituted a mess.

By the time you were five, you moved up to feeding chickens and gathering eggs. The feeding part was easy. You simply filled a pail in the granary and scattered the oats around the chicken yard, watching in amazement as the hens and a couple cocky roosters rushed to pick up the kernels. Gathering eggs in the henhouse, however, had its hazards. A pesky hen sometimes pecked your hand when you reached under her. She attacked so quick you didn't see her coming. One moment, the hen sat quietly on her nest; the next moment, she struck your hand with her power-ful beak, sometimes drawing blood and always causing pain, to say nothing of the scare. Not a pleasant experience. You had two choices: leave sitting hens alone and take eggs only from vacant nests—this was my strategy at first—or take your chances with a pecking hen. As I grew older, I grew braver. I talked to the hens, I must confess, in not the most endearing voice.

"Listen, hen, you peck me on the hand and I'll give you a whack alongside the head." I don't know if the threats worked or if I simply had less fear and the hen sensed it, because I received a lot less pecks as the years passed.

The ultimate chores took place in the cow barn. Milking cows by hand ranked number one. Other prestigious chores included forking hay from the haymow in ten-below-zero temperature, with frost hanging from the cobwebs and brushing you in the face; shoveling manure from the barn gutters into the manure carrier; cleaning out the calf pen; and throwing silage down from the top of the silo. These high-level chores provided bragging rights among your friends at the country school and with your city cousins.

My brothers and I were born on the farm, as the nearest hospital was forty miles away. A doctor from Wautoma assisted in the births, along with a neighbor woman, Augusta Miller, who served as midwife to many mothers in our neighborhood. We grew up calling our folks Ma and Pa—no Mom and Dad, Mother and Father, or Mommy and Daddy business. Those titles were used by city kids. Donald was called Duck (as in Donald Duck), and Darrel was called Murf (for his love of potatoes, or "murphies"). Ma and Pa raised us to work together, play together, and live to-gether. We helped each other, depended on each other, and at times defended each other, such as when a school bully picked on Duck or Murf.

My brothers and I also scrapped and argued and tried to best each other, to the utter dismay of our folks. "Would you kids quit bickering?" Ma often asked. We heard her, sort of. But when Pa said quit, we quit. He knew where the "lickin' stick" was, and the threat of its use stopped many an argument, especially those that resulted in some homegrown wrestling.

Everyone in our family contributed to the workload. Our mother, like farm women for a hundred years before her, washed and ironed clothes; canned fruits, vegetables, and meat; cooked meals; kept the big old drafty farmhouse in order; took care of the chickens; looked after the garden; and lorded over her big patch of strawberries. The egg and strawberry money were hers and hers alone. She used most of the money to buy clothes for us kids, home furnishings, Christmas presents, and greeting cards. She was forever sending birthday cards, sympathy cards, and get-well cards to relatives and friends near and far.

Chores were an important part of our growing up years. Pa and Ma had a wonderful "psychology" of chores. By this, I mean they introduced chores in such a way that we looked forward to doing the more difficult and time-consuming ones, such as milking cows by hand; new chores were a reward for having done lower level chores well. Pa's psychology was especially well developed. "You should be proud that you have chores to do," Pa often said. "Look what city kids are missing." Along with this psychology came several unspoken rules.

Though I sometimes wondered just what city kids were missing, now when I look back at chores, several lessons come to mind. We learned how to do a job well. We learned not to complain about work. We learned to show up on time, every time, day in and day out, including weekends. And we took pride in what we were doing. Chores were not drudgery, at least not on the farm where I grew up.

Farm work differed from chores. Farm work followed the seasons, particularly planting, growing, and harvesting seasons. Planting season opened with Pa plowing the field, a process that unearthed hundreds of stones, all of which had to be picked before crops could be planted. By the time you were six or seven, you helped pick the smaller stones. After the stones were picked, the fields were leveled by a team of horses pulling a disk harrow. This was followed by a fine-tooth drag that further smoothed the field. When you were ten or twelve, you drove the team while sitting on the disk harrow or you walked behind the drag while a dust cloud swirled around you.

Growing season meant hoeing corn and potatoes from the time you could walk (or so it seemed). You became a serious hoer when you were seven or eight—though it was hard to be serious about one of the farm's most boring, never-ending jobs. Pa always hoed with you, to set an example and to keep you on task. By age twelve or so, you were cultivating potatoes with one horse and a walking cultivator. This job involved holding a curved cultivator handle in each hand and, with the horse reins around your shoulders, steering a several-shoveled cultivator between the potato rows. The cultivator rooted out weeds; those it didn't remove, it buried. Cultivating was hard work, but considerably higher level than lowly hoeing.

Harvesting season began in July with haymaking. At age eight or nine, you helped bunch loose hay so Pa could fork it onto a horse-drawn hay wagon. By the time you were ten, you were driving the horses and performing simple tasks like handling the team while Pa pitched hay. When you were twelve or so, you were pitching hay along with Pa. Harvesting continued into September with threshing, when a crew traveled from farm to farm in the neighborhood. Men carried bags of grain from the threshing machine to the granary and dumped their bags out in the front of the grain bin. You started out at age eight or nine shoveling the dumped grain to the back of the bin. By the time you were fourteen, you were driving a team on the threshing crew. Harvesting wound down in October, when, by age twelve, you husked corn by hand for the hogs after school, often a wagonload every afternoon.

Winter farm work meant "making wood," which consisted of sawing down oak trees, limbing the downed trees, cutting the wood into manageable lengths, and toting the cut wood to the farmstead with a team and bobsled. Two or three times during the winter, Guy York, a neighbor with a large circle saw, came by for a sawing bee. After York sliced the wood into stove-length pieces, most still required splitting into a size that would fit into the kitchen woodstove. Splitting wood was a gray area, falling neither into the category of farm work or chores. Making wood was dangerous and Pa kept you away from helping until you were twelve or older. Then he introduced you to the job by teaching you how to use a splitting maul. Splitting wood, as Pa taught the skill, was more art than brute strength. It didn't matter how hard you struck the chunk of wood but where you struck it. In Pa's words, you had to "read the wood." (It took me most of a winter to figure out what he meant.)

All this and much more was farm work. Chores were done in the morning and the evening, after the farm work was done.

As to any money we received, Pa gave me and my brothers each a dime on Saturday night, just before we went to town. With five cents, I could buy a double-dip strawberry ice cream cone and an immense Hershey candy bar, with or without nuts and divided into neat squares that could be broken off and eaten one at a time. In the summer, we also drove to town on Tuesday evenings to see the free outdoor movies. Pa advised us to save some of the ten cents we got on Saturday night for Tuesday night popcorn.

Relatives often gave us cash on our birthdays—fifty cents and sometimes even a dollar from a city aunt. We were strongly urged to save this unearned money. Pa helped me start a postal saving account at the Wild Rose Post Office—interest at 2 percent.

Our major source of income came from picking potatoes in the fall—one cent for each bushel picked. The country school gave "potato vacation" so all the children could stay home and help with the potato crop. Some vacation! But working behind two sturdy men digging potatoes with six-tine forks, I could pick one hundred bushels a day and earn one dollar. I purchased my first .22 rifle with potato-picking money.

Our second major income source came from picking cucumbers and green beans in the summer. Pa usually grew an acre of each crop, and we could keep the money earned from selling the cukes and beans we picked. Sometimes we would pocket five dollars or more from a day's work. Most of this went into the savings account. "Never can tell when you might need the money," Pa often said.

Pa had known good times and bad. "One always follows the other," he would say. "But sometimes you don't know when times are bad, until they're really bad. That's why you need some savings to tide you over until the good times roll around again."

By the time I was twelve, I put every nickel I earned toward buying books. (I didn't yet understand Pa's good times–bad times theory.) Forty-nine cents bought a hardcover copy of *Treasure Island, The Black Arrow, Swiss Family Robinson,* or other such classics.

As I look back on those years, I realize that Pa and Ma made absolutely clear what was important in their lives. I never doubted what they valued or what they wanted their boys to value. Family came first, then neighbors, the farm, the barn and other outbuildings, the milk cows, the team of horses (later a tractor), our farm dog Fanny, the well (good water was invaluable), good fences, a big garden, our farm house, and, finally, the 1936 Plymouth car.

Some of what Pa and Ma valued was more subtle. As I recall, Pa valued silence, darkness, knee-high corn, sunrise and sunset, animals both tame and wild, a walk in the woods, baby kittens, wildflowers, freshly mown hay, a snowstorm, newly plowed soil, country roads, a rainy day, melting snow, and a good story.

Ma valued a clean house, her church, a well-kept parlor, a good canning season, favorable garden weather, the coming of spring, her boys doing well in school, her flowers, her chicken flock, and homebaked bread.

Ma and Pa also taught us to value our own conduct. These values, often unspoken, translated into a deep-rooted sense of ethics. Farmers in my community didn't talk about values; they lived them. You could see their values come through every day in their respect for the land, their compassion for their neighbors, and their love for their families.

RULES FOR CHORES

- Perform your chores so well that you will have the opportunity to move up to more challenging ones.

- Never complain about your chores, no matter what the weather or what else you would prefer to do at the time.

- Never miss your chores. (No one discussed the consequences of missing chores, because the imagined punishment was too frightful.)

- Negotiate with a brother to do your chores if you can not—if he is capable of doing the chore.

- Feel free to brag about doing chores when talking to your city cousins. (This was one of the few times bragging was permissible.)

MA AND PA'S ETHICS

- Never boast.

- Consider being able to work hard a blessing.

- Remember your name; once it is tarnished it will remain so.

- Be thankful for what you have, even when others have more.

- Remember that next year will be better.

- Walk whenever possible.

- Accept those different from you.

- Save your money.

- Never stop learning.

- Appreciate your friends; good friends are worth more than a bulging bank account.

- Realize that joy can be found almost everywhere, if you take time to look.

- Care for others, especially those who have less than you.

- Pay cash for what you buy, except for land.

- Know the power of place and the joy of belonging.

- Maintain a sense of cheerfulness even when sadness surrounds you.

- Never forget that laughter and humor will trump grumpiness and seriousness every time.

- Keep things simple; there is great truth in simplicity.

- Love the land; it is the foundation of everything.

~

CHAPTER 2

One Hundred Sixty Acres
of Stones and Hills

Welding and repairing plow points—$4.50

Our farmland was both hilly and stony. The hills were embedded with big stones and little stones; jagged stones and smooth, nearly round stones; red stones, gray stones, black stones, and speckled stones. Some of the stones were tiny and colorful. Others were large and ugly. The largest were as big as a draft horse and far heavier. These we left in the field and worked around. The rest we picked up and moved to the fence lines.

The stones were deposited in the land ten thousand years ago. That was when the last great glacier that had slowly ground across Wisconsin began to recede. As the glacier melted, it dumped a load of debris on the land, creating what is called a terminal moraine. Our farm sat right dab in the middle of where this tremendous glacier quit. So the land was hilly, sharply so in places, and riddled with rocks.

Every spring, we picked all but the largest stones. The following fall, the plow dug up more stones. And over the winter, the cycle of freezing and thawing brought yet another crop of stones to the surface. Come the next spring, Pa disked the fields, then we'd be out there again, picking stones. When my brothers were old enough, they helped, too. Sometimes, stone picking coincided with our brief Easter vacation. Otherwise, Pa conveniently saved an ample amount of stone picking for Saturdays.

Before we owned a tractor, our team of horses dragged the stones off the fields. Pa hitched Frank and Charlie to a stone boat. A stone boat looked nothing like a boat. No one ever used it for fishing or took it to a lake. It consisted of white oak planks, two or more inches thick and sawed so the front curved up a few inches. It was probably eight feet long and forty inches wide. A white oak rim, two inches high, ran all around the boat, so the stones stayed in place when the boat was pulled.

Because I was older, I usually helped harness the team and hitch them to the stone boat. When we were ready, we all jumped on the boat, Pa said "Giddap" to the team, and we were off. Duck, Murf, and I quickly learned to stand with our feet apart and our knees bent so we didn't fall as the team walked smartly toward the oat field, dragging the stone boat across the ground.

Once in the field, we lugged stones to the boat and rolled those we couldn't carry. For the stones we couldn't roll by ourselves, we worked cooperatively, although we often accused a brother of not doing his fair share of pushing. We shoveled around particularly difficult stones to make them easier to move. And we used a crowbar to edge larger stones toward and finally onto the stone boat.

Occasionally, we encountered a stone that wouldn't budge with any of these procedures.

"Unhitch the team," Pa would say. I unhitched Frank and Charlie from the stone boat, and Pa drove them around to the balky rock. The horses were still harnessed to a doubletree, a hickory crossbar that harnesses two draft animals side by side. We hooked a logging chain around the stone and then to the doubletree and had the horses drag the stone off the field. Pa taught me how to hook the chain so that it didn't come undone.

The trick was to fasten the chain around the stone in such a way that the horses had a chance to turn the stone to start it moving.

When the stone boat was heaped high with stones, Pa whistled to the team and we dragged the load to the nearest "shore." We used that language when we were hauling with the stone boat, maybe to be consistent. We tossed the stones in huge piles at the edge of the field, or shore.

Picking stones left me exhausted, covered with dust and dirt from head to toe, and so hungry it seemed like I hadn't eaten for days. I declared it the worst job on the farm, even worse than hoeing.

After many years of stone picking, the stone piles along the edges of particularly stony fields became quite a sight. Here were a myriad of colors, brown and red, purple and gray, white and black, and even some green where moss had grown on the stones. All sizes, too, from stones the size of baseballs to a few so large I could remember the story of moving them off the field. We were proud of these piles, from purely a work-accomplished perspective. We could stand back of a stone pile and say, "I helped build that." Stone picking was one of those jobs where you could clearly see the results of your labors. Anyone who had ever picked stones would look at a stone pile, whistle under his breath, and shake his head. He didn't have to say anything, because stone-pickers shared the knowledge of the work involved.

Stone piles were attractive for other reasons, too. As much as we cussed the stones and deplored the work involved in moving them, a stone pile was a beautiful thing. It was like a huge sculpture of shape and color, of the earth and blending with the earth. We hesitated to admit it, but our stone piles belonged. They looked like they were meant to be there.

Sometimes, in a larger field, we built a stone pile in the middle of the field—not just anywhere, but around a boulder that couldn't be moved or in a gully that couldn't be plowed. These piles saved us travel time to the far "shores." Piling stones in gullies also slowed down gushing water and prevented the gully from growing larger. In March, after a couple days of thaw, I often walked out to the field northeast of the farmstead. We had tossed stones in a gully here for years. It had long ceased to be an erosion threat, but water still ran through the gully. One of the thrills of spring was seeing running water again, after months of ice and snow. The stone pile in the gully added yet another dimension as the water gurgled through the stones. To hear spring coming was as much a thrill as seeing it.

After a morning of stone picking, tracks made by the stone boat crisscrossed the oat field, a rather pleasant sight. I liked to imagine some huge, unknown reptile had made the tracks by crawling on its belly all around the field, up the hills and down, searching for food. Other times I imagined the tracks were roads, little highways that ran all around the field with no particular destination in mind. Sometimes I would run along them; the packed soil made running easy compared to the rest of the field's soft, dusty soil.

After a few days of stone picking, we moved on to other farm tasks that required far less lifting and were less dirty. But stone picking, finished for one season, was never done. Just as spring came each year, so did stone picking.

Of course, the plow usually found the stones first, especially those that hadn't yet broken the surface. When plowing with a team and a one-bottom walking plow, I learned to keep the plow handles out in front of me. I wrapped the harness lines around my shoulders, freeing my hands to hold the plow handles. If I weren't careful, I'd be moving along just fine, enjoying the smell of freshly turned soil, appreciating the hardworking, sweaty team out in front of me, when, without warning, the plow would hit a stone and leap out of the ground, slamming me in the side. A careful plowman working a stony field was always alert.

Sometimes when you hit a stone head-on, nothing budged—except the plow point. Broken harness leather was also common when plowing stony ground.

Some say that working stony ground builds character, that it makes farmers strong. My take is that it creates a farmer who constantly thinks about buying a different farm, one that is stone free. The sickening thud made when farm machinery collides with a stone is one of the farmer's most dreaded sounds. It usually means a trip to town with a broken part, hours of farm time gone, and a bit of religion lost.

Pa always said to make the most of what you have and try to see the good within the bad. Hard to find much good in a stony field—except maybe the gurgle of melt water rushing through stones in a gulley on an early spring day.

CHAPTER 3

-~

The Neighborhood

Staples—$.63
Roll of barbed wire—$8.00

We called our farm community Chain O' Lake, after the Chain
O' Lake School located a mile from our farm. This unusual name
contradicted itself. One would ordinarily see Chain O' Lakes, but
we used the singular "lake." The name came from a small lake a
third of a mile south of the school. Chain O' Lake was freestand-
ing, but another lake stood just over the hill, and another lake
stood over the next hill, and yet another one over the hill beyond
that. The unattached lineup of lakes did not form a chain, yet they
stood close enough that some wag decided on the name "Chain
O' Lake."

In some ways, our community's name symbolized other
contradictory dimensions in our neighborhood, ranging from
religion to ethnicity, from hardworking farmers to those who
worked as little as possible, from honest and upstanding citizens
to thieves and deadbeats.

In the years during and just after World War II, our neighborhood included many farms, some as small as eighty acres, but
most one hundred sixty acres—a quarter section. This was the
standard size for Midwestern farms, following the survey that divided the land into townships, then sections and quarter sections.

Farmers considered a quarter section about the right size for a family farm when the land was worked with horses, and family members provided the labor.

Our neighbors within two miles or so of the Chain O' Lake schoolhouse included seven Germans (William Witt—my grandfather, William Miller, Miles Buelow, Paul Krueger, Fred Rapp, and Arlin Handrich), six Englishmen (MacKinley Jenks, John Coombes, Floyd Jeffers, Mortimer Oliphant, Jesse DeWitt, and Guy York), five Poles (Otto Gabrilski, John Swendryzinski, Clint Hudziak, Fred Gabrilski, and Paul Sjcybulewski), three Welshmen (Alan Davis, Albert Davis, and Griff Davis), one Norwegian (Vilas Olson), and one Bohemian (Frank Kolka). Almost all were first- or second-generation immigrants. My father, Herman Apps, was second-generation German and English.

In addition to representing several ethnic groups, our neighborhood had multiple religions. The Germans and Norwegians tended to be Lutheran (Missouri Synod and Norwegian Lutheran); the Welsh, Presbyterian; the English, Methodist and Baptist; and the Polish, Catholic. Several neighbors attended no church.

Whenever one of the churches held a fundraiser—a harvest dinner, bake sale, polka dance (popular with the Catholic church in the small crossroad community of Heffron)—everyone in the community attended, no matter what faith they professed. Same for weddings and funerals. Neighbors went their separate religious ways, yet they supported each other's churches. They had to, because no congregation had enough people to go it alone.

Neighbors relentlessly flung ethnic slurs—"Polack," "Bohunk," "Norski," and "Kraut"—but usually without malice. When they gathered for school programs, threshing, wood sawing, silo filling, or corn shredding, they good-naturedly teased each other about their respective religions, especially the Protestants and the Catholics. The Protestants teased the Catholics about their Latin services and no meat on Fridays. The Catholics got on the Baptists because they wouldn't allow their children to attend the free movies. (The Baptists believed movies to be tools of the devil.) Everyone agreed that the Welsh Presbyterian church had the best singers. In fact, for a period of time, Everett Jones, the undertaker in Wild Rose, a Welshman and a Presbyterian, provided complete services for many funerals in the community, from preparing the body for burial to singing a solo at the funeral. The Methodists were applauded because if someone needed to be married, buried, or baptized, they would do it, even if the person had seldom darkened the doorstep of the Methodist church, or any other church for that matter.

Underneath the religious and ethnic tolerance was the simple truth that our community of farmers got along not because it was good or right, but because it was necessary. Farmers in the mid-1900s needed each other to survive. Farmers had strong independent tendencies, but they possessed equally strong feelings about community. Work such as threshing, silo filling, and wood sawing could not be accomplished by the farm family alone. Every family needed outside help, and the "bee" was all-important. A threshing bee, a wood-sawing bee, or a quilting bee meant neighbors exchanged work to get the job done. No money ever changed hands.

Every farm community had a collection of specialists who were especially good at some necessary task. In our neighborhood, Bill Miller was an excellent butcher, Alan Davis was a fine carpenter, and Pa knew how to castrate pigs and how to set and splint an animal's broken leg. I learned how to splice together hayfork ropes—the thick rope used with a special hayfork to pull loose hay from a wagon into the barn—when they broke. When one of the neighbors needed help with a particular task, he knew who to call.

Neighbors also provided quick emergency help. Volunteer fire departments did not venture outside the village limits, leaving farm communities on their own when disaster hit. If lightning struck a farmhouse, if a bull gored a farmhand, if a tornado toppled a barn, if a child took ill—a quick phone call, and help was immediately at hand. Farm people relied on the party-line telephone to summon their neighbors. A series of short rings meant someone needed help. No matter what a person was doing when he heard the general ring, he stopped doing it and headed to the farm in question. Within a few minutes, the neighbor in trouble had a yard full of farmers. Depending on the seriousness of the emergency—a barn fire, for instance—the farmwives would follow with food for the emergency crew.

The farmers in our community also needed their neighbors as a social outlet, especially during the long, cold winter months when the days were short and often without sun. Loneliness was a regular visitor to isolated farm families. We traveled to neighboring farmhouses to play cards, attend dances, or just to visit, often walking through the snow and the dark. In the days before electricity, if a radio battery died, a farmer might walk a mile to his neighbor's house to hear his favorite radio program. No one wanted to miss the Friday night prize fights or the world news.

Farmwives often gathered during winter for quilting bees. Sometimes, a quilt stretched on a quilt rack in our dining room for weeks, with women stopping by several times until it was finished. Of course, they stitched all the needlework by hand.

The Chain O' Lake schoolhouse served as the social hub of the community, where we held dances, birthday parties, and anniversary gatherings, in addition to school-sponsored events such as Halloween, Christmas, and Valentine programs, plus the always popular end-of-school-year picnic.

Our community, like many farm communities then and now, had homegrown musicians. Frank Kolka played the concertina, Pinky Eserhut played the banjo, and Harry Banks fiddled.

Although none read music, they entertained at many school and community gatherings. It was impossible to measure the worth of these three musicians, who provided a brief respite from thoughts of overdue mortgage payments, rationing, sick cows, miserably long winters, and a war that seemed to go on forever.

Several of our neighbors were storytellers, my father included. He recounted tales of earlier days with color and dialogue that kept everyone interested and laughing. One of our neighbors was known to exaggerate. But most of us, especially the kids, didn't care if the story was truth or fiction as long as it was well told.

Sometimes, Pa's stories were just plain funny, at least for farm kids accustomed to the gravity of the Depression and World War II.

"Hear about the two farmers in Waupaca County?" Pa would begin.

Someone always said, "Nope, don't believe so."

"Well, one claimed to have chickens that gave such big eggs that it required only one egg for baking a cake. He bragged about his chickens everywhere he went, until one day, he was telling this second farmer about it. Second farmer looked him right in the eye and said, 'I got hens like that. Fact is they lay such big eggs it takes only nine to make a dozen.'"

Those were the stories that got us through the long Waushara County winters.

Like every collection of human beings, not everyone in our neighborhood got along. But because we depended on each other so much, we put aside a dispute—petty or serious—when we needed neighborhood cooperation.

Over the years, we learned that three of our neighbors were thieves. They stole tools from implements, such as mowers and grain binders, left out in the field; they took small tools from tool sheds; and once, one even stole our baby kittens. The thefts occurred only once or twice a year, but almost every farmer lost something to these thieves. Word was they even stole small things from each other. To my knowledge, no one ever called the sheriff to report these thefts, even the time a stolen tool was found a few days later at the culprit's farm. No matter what a neighbor had done, we ultimately overlooked almost every offense with the phrase, "After all, they are our neighbors."

But there were limits. One dark night in the fall, a farmer on the fringe of our neighborhood walked into a neighbor's henhouse and sacked up a bunch of laying hens. This time the victim called the sheriff, and the thief spent a year in jail. Stealing a bunch of chickens stepped over the line. So did stealing a bin-full of freshly threshed wheat or a tank of gas. Pa would have called the sheriff had he found out which neighbor emptied our grain bin while we were away at the county fair, or which one drained the gasoline from the gas tank back of the corncrib.

But even "crooked" neighbors were called on in an emergency. On the farm, being a neighbor went well beyond merely living in the same area.

As part of our neighborly duties, Pa and I regularly walked the fences surrounding our farm, carrying a hammer, some staples, and a few feet of barbed wire. We replaced broken posts and repaired broken wire. Keeping good fences was important. We didn't want our livestock to get out, nor did we want our neighbors' livestock to come in. We made the two-mile hike about once a month in summer.

Neighbors shared this duty. For instance, if a half mile of fence separated two farms, you took responsibility for one quarter mile of fence, and your neighbor took responsibility for the other quarter mile. It made for another interesting contradiction: If you fell back on your duty to your own fence, you stood to irritate your neighbor.

The old saying "Good fences make good neighbors" contains more than a little truth.

↬

CHAPTER 4

War

Living-room suite—$95.00
Living-room rug—$40.00
Wallpaper—$1.46
Wall paint—$1.00
Four pairs of curtains—$4.00
Four window shades—$2.75

During the war years, Ma decided it was time for some new home furnishings. She purchased a living-room suite—a large, rose-colored sofa and matching rose-colored stuffed chairs. The price, ninety-five dollars, was a lot of money in 1942. In today's dollars, the suite would cost more than fourteen hundred dollars.

The furniture went into the parlor, along with a matching rose-patterned wool rug. Ma also bought paint and wallpaper, new curtains, and window shades, all to spruce up the parlor. We seldom used this room in the summer and never in the winter, as Ma closed it off from the heat. The parlor's main purpose, it seemed, was to impress our city relatives who occasionally visited in the summer. They never showed up in winter for fear a snowstorm would strand them and they'd be forced to use the outhouse and kerosene lamps.

World War II had a definite upside for farmers. Coming on the heels of the Great Depression, the war dramatically increased prices for farm produce. The federal government created the Office of Price Administration (OPA) to control the prices of goods and prevent wartime inflation. Prices charged in March 1942 became the ceiling prices for most commodities, but not for milk, meat, and other farm produce. The prices of farm products, which had been forced down by the long, devastating Depression, rose during the war years. For the past decade, farmers, along with everyone else, had struggled to earn enough money to make mortgage payments and avoid bankruptcy. Pa certainly belonged to that group.

When the stock market crashed in 1929, Pa was renting the home farm from a landlord named John R. Jones. Rent was one-third of the farm income, and Pa furnished everything. Eight years later, Pa managed to buy the farm for four thousand six hundred dollars with a mortgage at 3 percent interest. With backing from Emmett Humphrey, a lawyer friend in Wautoma, Pa purchased the farm for one dollar down. Taxes were sixty-five dollars a year and interest was one hundred thirty-eight dollars a year.

The price of milk, our primary income source, more than doubled during the war. Ma's record books show that, in January 1938, milk fetched $1.20 per hundredweight, and milk sales earned us $10.76 over a two-week period. By January 1942, our two-week income had increased nearly threefold—up to $31.68. By January 1945, milk prices had risen to $2.48 per hundredweight; with Pa and me milking even more cows on the newly purchased milking machine, our two-week income was up to $100.52.

The war also boosted the price of pork. In fact, hogs became known as "mortgage lifters." That was surely true on our farm. We had always raised pigs, mostly Chester Whites and Berkshires. Just before the war, pork sold for around six dollars a hundred pounds. One year into the war and it was selling for ten dollars a hundred. By the middle years of the war, Pa sold as many as a hundred pigs a year and earned enough to pay off the farm's mortgage.

With a little extra money, Ma decided the house needed
sprucing up. Before the war, the farm scarcely earned enough
income to pay the mortgage interest, and now we had money to
spend on home improvements—the last place farmers in those
years spent money. Ma had likely been harping on Pa for house
money ever since milk prices rose.

But not all the farm's disposable income went to the parlor. Pa
made some major purchases as well. He bought a twenty-four-
dollar hay mower, a sixty-five-dollar disc harrow, and two new
plow points for $1.30 each. But mostly he paid to have things
fixed so they would continue operating until the war was over. Ex-
amples: work on wagon tongue—$1.75; repairing plow—$2.50;
repairing mower—$7.05 (struck a stone while mowing); and
repairing plow points—$2.50 (struck many stones).

In 1943, Ma continued making purchases that I'm sure had
been put off. Even with rationing, and limited supplies of almost
everything in the Wild Rose stores, she noted the following purchases in her account book.

January 9	Two shirts for twins $.79 each	$1.58
January 9	Gloves for Herm	$.52
January 11	Shoes for Donald and Darrell	$4.25
January 12	School bag for Jerold	$.88
February 17	Clothes for myself	$4.25
February 17	Overalls for Herm	$3.25
March 4	Shirt for Herm	$1.49
March 5	Overalls for boys (4 pairs)	$3.56
March 12	Milk pail	$1.15
March 16	Horse collar	$7.50
March 13	Shoes for Jerold	$2.90
March 21	Curtains	$4.50
May 2	Lawn mower	$15.90

Every farmer wants a well-tended farmstead, with painted buildings, a tidy fence, and a mowed lawn. But during the Depression,
saving the farm took top priority. The grass grew long on the hill
in front of the farmhouse. The hill, scattered with a couple apple
trees and a big red pine Pa had planted, sloped from the house
down to the country road. Pa rarely even considered mowing it.
Once or twice a summer, when he was mowing hay, he might
drive the team across the grass for a quick swipe. But mostly Pa
ignored the lawn.

Now, with more farm income, Pa spent money on a new
barnyard fence, paint for the fence and the barn, and a push
lawn mower. And he added another job to my brothers' and my
chores—mowing the lawn. Pa figured for the lawn mower to do
a good job the metal reel, when it turned, should firmly strike
the stationary cutting bar. The tighter the adjustment of reel to
cutting bar, the harder to push the lawn mower. Pa's theory was
probably correct, but pushing the mower was near impossible for
one person, especially a nine-year-old boy.

But Pa was firm. We had a lawn mower and the lawn would be
cut, about once a week in early summer, less often as the summer
wore on. My brothers and I worked out a system. We tied a shank
of rope to the mower handle. To mow, I pushed while my brothers
pulled on the rope in front of the mower. Mowing became one of
the worst jobs on the farm, up there with picking stones, hoeing
thistles in the hollows, and forking manure from the calf pens.

That summer, Pa painted the barn red and the new fence
white. Our farmstead, once rather ordinary in appearance, leapt
to the top in the neighborhood. All because the war improved
milk and hog prices and OPA kept a lid on costs.

But OPA also rationed the distribution of goods we needed
to purchase—including sugar, coffee, meat, cheese, butter, shoes,
tires, and gasoline. We lived with ration books, stamps, tokens,
and coupons. Some restrictions affected us very little, others a

great deal. Our hogs provided plenty of meat, and our dairy cows some butter, though we used it only on special occasions. Ma considered butter too expensive for everyday use when we could make do with melted lard. No automobiles or new tractors were available, so few farmers complained about the lack of gasoline. Pa received an allotment of gas for farm use in our old home-made tractor, which we could have used in our 1936 Plymouth car—who would know?—but we couldn't buy tires for the car. We rarely traveled much farther than Wild Rose or Wautoma.

The sugar rationing hit us the hardest. Ma learned how to bake and cook with substitutes such as sorghum, Karo corn syrup, and honey. We grew our own sorghum, which tasted something like molasses but was not as dark or strong tasting. Sorghum had a more pronounced flavor than Karo syrup, which we used to sweeten our breakfast cereal. The syrup stuck the cornflakes or oatmeal together in globs that made our food not only unsightly but difficult to eat.

The honey came from our Uncle Ed's several beehives. The government gave him a special allotment of sugar to feed his bees over the winter. He fed the bees the bare minimum of sugar and distributed the rest among his relatives—his sisters Elsie, Minnie, Doris, and Irene, and his brothers Herman, John, Fred, and George. Problem was he had so many relatives there was not enough sugar for either the relatives or the bees.

War shortages also halted the stringing of electric lines in Waushara County. Back in 1936, the Rural Electrification Admin-istration legislation had passed Congress, and the REA electric co-op had begun stringing lines in our community in the late 1930s. The REA strung lines within a mile of our farm before it stopped. Thus, we farmed through the war years as we had for the past fifty years—with kerosene lamps and lanterns for light, and a gasoline engine to power the water pump that supplied fresh water to our dairy cattle.

My grandfather Witt's farm, along County Highway A, was among those hooked up to electricity just before the war started. He owned a Delco electrical system, which included a gasoline-powered generator and a pump house half filled with huge glass batteries. The 32-volt system provided minimum lighting, power to operate a washing machine, and current for an iron. When we visited our grandparents, we were constantly amazed at "how good they had it" with this fancy, home-produced electrical system.

Our neighbor Andrew Nelson also had an electrical generator, but his was powered by a "wind charger," a large windmill with three long blades. The problem with Nelson's system was no wind, no electricity. Of course, batteries stored some of the energy the generator produced, but a couple of calm days and the Nelsons were back with the rest of us, using kerosene lanterns.

Our city relatives couldn't understand why we didn't complain more about not having electricity. The answer was simple. When you are accustomed to something—when you haven't directly experienced something better—you have no basis for complaint. Our kerosene lamps and lanterns, gasoline engines, and wood stoves served us fine. In a way, we took pride in our independence. Neighbors told tales of storms knocking down electric lines and thrusting farms into darkness. No matter how fierce the storm, our lights always worked.

When Ma's relatives visited from Wisconsin Rapids in summer 1942, they gushed about the fine new living-room suite. The parlor served as a "showplace" to let Ma's urban relatives know we weren't in such dire poverty we couldn't afford fancy furniture and a wool rug, complete with a fiber pad. Pa held his tongue. He would rather have used the money on farm machinery. Besides, he didn't care for this branch of Ma's relatives. The men all worked in the paper mills on the Wisconsin River. The loud factory noises had turned the older ones deaf as stumps, and none seemed to have much to say about anything, except for a comment or two about the inconvenience of rationing. One of Ma's cousins was so boring that after a big noon meal he slumped down in one of the rose-colored chairs for an hour, snoring briskly as the rest tried to carry on some semblance of reasonable conversation.

That summer, Ma required us to appear before the relatives to illustrate how much we had grown, and how little we had suffered from war rationing. She then released us from the wrath of the relatives to play outside, away from cigar and pipe smoke, away from the smells of new furniture, away from the parlor where if we spilled anything we were in deep trouble. Outdoors, the smells were fresh and clean, of cows and pastures, green grass and oak woods. We ran and jumped and fell down—and spilled things if we wanted to, without anyone so much as noticing.

The truth is that World War II touched everyone—rural and urban, young and old. We all knew men who were fighting. My uncle Ed's sons, Vernon, Ellsworth, and Ronald; my Uncle Fred's son, Bernard; my Uncle John's son, Kermit—all fighting the war. And our neighbor boys, Miles Buelow and Roman Macijeski, were away fighting.

We received news about World War II several ways: from the day-late *Milwaukee Sentinel* that appeared six days a week in our mailbox, about eleven o'clock each morning; from the radio, especially national radio commentator Gabriel Heater's reports; and by word of mouth from the men who gathered at the gristmill, at Christensen's Blacksmith Shop, and around the woodstove in back of Hotz's Hardware in Wild Rose.

In early January 1945, I was nine years old and the Battle of the Bulge dominated the news. It had begun on December 16, 1944, and would continue to January 28, 1945. The *Milwaukee Sentinel* reported that more than a million men fought in that battle: 600,000 Germans, 500,000 Americans, and 55,000 British. The causalities were enormous: United States, 81,000 injured, with

19,000 dead; British, 1,400 injured, with 200 dead; and 100,000 German soldiers killed, wounded, or captured.

Arnold Christensen kept a huge map of Europe posted on the dirty, gray, wooden wall of his blacksmith shop. His son was fighting in the war, so Arnold followed closely the American advance, battles won and battles lost, and young men killed. Pa and I stopped in his shop often that winter, and it was always warm. Not only was a big woodstove going, but the forge, where Arnold heated his metals, glowed orange through the smoke and dust.

"This is where they are now," Arnold said as he brushed black soot from the map.

CHAPTER 5

Winter

Overshoes for the twins—$2.78
Shoes for the twins—$4.25
Shoes for Jerold—$2.50
Mittens for Jerold—$.59

Pa said a storm was coming. If we hustled, my brothers and I could walk the mile from our farm to the Chain O' Lake School in fifteen minutes. The trek took longer if we climbed the snowbanks or dragged our sleds along, but we left our sleds home today because Pa said the storm would keep us inside during noon break and afternoon recess. Pa had an uncanny ability to predict weather change. No matter what the season, he was usually right.

As Duck, Murf, and I headed out, snow drifted over the high banks lining the country road. The school was located at the bottom of Miller's Hill, where County Highway A and our country road intersected. The twins were in third grade, and I was in seventh. Several feet of snow covered the fields; it had begun falling in November and hadn't let up yet. Every week seemed to bring another storm, usually accompanied by wind and snowdrifts. The snowplow had piled the snow so high along both sides of our road that it was like walking in a trench. In a few places, if we stood on the snowbanks, we could touch the telephone wires.

When we reached the top of Miller's Hill, the school bell announced it was eight-thirty. School started at nine, so we had plenty of time to toss clumps of snow at each other and enjoy the pleasant winter morning.

The schoolhouse was a big white building with a bell tower on the roof. When we arrived, we put our lard-pail lunch buckets on the entryway shelf, hung our wool mackinaw coats and caps on nearby hooks, and greeted our teacher, Miss Thompson. She had arrived an hour earlier to start a fire in the big, rusty woodstove in back, so the building would be reasonably warm when we arrived.

At nine o'clock, an eighth grader gave a couple long pulls on the bell rope in the entryway, telling us it was time for school to start. We stood, said the Pledge of Allegiance, and another school day began. In warmer weather, we gathered around the flagpole outside, stood witness to the raising of the flag, and recited the pledge when the flag reached the top. But through the coldest winter months, an eighth grader simply hooked the flag on the rope, raised the flag into place, and hurried back into the warm schoolhouse.

The first snowflakes fell during morning recess; Pa's prediction had been a couple hours off. We were outside playing fox and geese on the circular track that we had pounded into the snow several days earlier. The flakes were tiny, like specks of dandruff falling off an unseen giant's head. We scarcely noticed them as we played. By the time the recess bell rang, signaling our return to the schoolroom, the wind had picked up and the snowflakes were larger and accumulating. We piled back into the schoolhouse. Miss Thompson had a pan of water heating on the stovetop, and those of us with chili or soup in our lunches put the glass jars in the pan, so our food would be warm by noon. Miss Thompson always reminded us to loosen the covers so they wouldn't blow up, and she checked to make sure that we did. Just once it would have been fun to see a jar explode. Winter school days, especially in January, tended to be boring, and a small explosion might add a dollop of excitement.

With the snow falling and the wind rattling the windows, I had a hard time keeping my mind on seventh-grade geography, or arithmetic, or anything else. Even with all the inconvenience, an old-fashioned blizzard was exciting.

By noon, the snow fell so rapidly we could scarcely see the boy's toilet on the southwest corner of the school grounds. The girl's toilet was on the northwest corner. Winter visits to the outhouse were brief. In a raging snowstorm, they were even briefer. There was always the remote possibility that you would not find your way back in the storm. At times like this, Miss Thompson volunteered an older student to accompany the younger ones. This was an important duty that older students begrudgingly accepted.

On a regular school day, Miss Thompson dismissed class at three o'clock and we headed home on our own. But a snowstorm was different. At two-thirty, the fathers began arriving to walk their children home. One after the other they came, stomping the snow from their six-buckle overshoes. Some had walked more than two miles. Not only had the intensity of the snow and wind increased, the temperature had fallen, too, so the walk home would be a miserable one. As the fathers gathered around the woodstove, we put away our books and papers. The men compared snow depths and wind intensity as they stood rubbing their big calloused hands together in front of the stove.

My brothers and I pulled on our mackinaws and overshoes, put the earflaps down on our caps, and wrapped our scarves around our faces so just our eyes showed. We started for home, up Miller's long hill. Pa walked first, breaking a trail. A foot of new snow had already accumulated, and in some places, the wind had swept thigh-high drifts across the road. Duck followed second, trying to step in Pa's tracks, Murf followed him, and I brought up the rear. Sometimes, the snow blew so thick, I could scarcely glimpse Pa in the lead. At times, when the wind caught us, it took our breath away and we had to turn our backs to it until we could breathe again. We'd walked for maybe a half hour before I glimpsed Bill Miller's farm buildings on the left, dimly silhouetted in the blowing snow. We were but halfway home. Step, lift your foot, step again, always staying in Pa's tracks, except when he forgets that his followers have much shorter legs.

I nearly fell over Murf when he stopped. Up ahead, Pa had announced we should rest for a few minutes. We stopped in the shelter of an enormous snowbank created by the snowplow. The blowing snow shot right over us. Sheltered from the wind, the stopping place was almost comfortable, except for the bitter cold. Snow covered each of us, from the tops of our scarf-wrapped heads to the tips of our four-buckle boots. Only our eyes peered out from the whiteness, and snow even covered our eyebrows.

Murf starred to sit down, but Pa said no.

"I'm tired," Murf complained. "I just want to rest."

"Got to keep goin'," Pa said. "No more restin' 'til we're home."

Pa had told stories many times of people walking in a blizzard who stopped to rest and froze to death. Sometimes they died within shouting distance of their homes. Pa's strategy was to rest just enough to catch your breath, and then trudge on, no matter how exhausted or cold you were.

We started walking again, slowly, deliberately, difficult step after difficult step, nothing to see but snow, snow in every direction—up, down, left, right. Snow everywhere. Wet, cold, stinging snow. Every step was agony. I was so tired and so cold. I began to wonder if we would make it home or if we would become part of that group that dies each year in a northern blizzard. The sun hadn't set, but the afternoon was near dark as night. Pa carried no lantern, but I knew that if he stayed within the snowbanks on either side of the road and we boys kept trudging on, following in his footsteps, that eventually—if exhaustion didn't overtake us first—we would reach home.

Then, finally, our barn appeared through the driving snow, and we quickened our steps. Within a few minutes, we were inside the house, peeling off our scarves, shaking off our mackinaws, and warming our hands over the kitchen woodstove. Ma had an enormous kettle of vegetable soup simmering on the back of the stove, and the smell of cooking vegetables permeated the entire house. The warm, steamy kitchen was a pleasant contrast to the frigid cold and driving snow just beyond the kitchen door.

Fanny, our farm dog, rose from the rug behind the stove and greeted each of us in turn. Ma allowed her in the house on stormy days. Fanny was a big collie, and when she wagged her tail against your leg, it felt like someone was whacking you with a stick, but we didn't mind because we knew it meant she was just happy to see us.

After a couple bowls of soup, I could barely keep my eyes open. The warmth of the kitchen and a full stomach after a cold walk had that effect. I noticed that my brothers could hardly keep their eyes open either.

Pa noticed, too. "Time to do the chores," he said as he pushed his chair back from the table. That was our signal to bundle up and feed the chickens, carry in wood, and—for me—trudge to the barn with Pa to do the evening milking.

With full stomachs and drooping eyes, my brothers and I forced ourselves up from the kitchen table. We pulled on our overshoes, slipped on our wet mackinaw jackets and caps, wrapped the damp scarves around our heads, and stepped back out into the storm, leaving behind the warmth of the kitchen. Our chores were waiting.

CHAPTER 6

At Home

Milk pail—$.89
Milk stool—$.59

Pa let loose a series of cusses as he milked the big rangy Holstein. She gave lots of milk but she was a "kicker," which meant she'd just as soon drive a hoof into your chest as look at you. Meanwhile, I mentally noted a new curse word to share next day at the country school.

Once you reached fifth grade, you were eligible to attend cussing lessons, which the eighth graders conducted back of the boy's outhouse. Hearing Pa milk this ornery cow enhanced my cussing language to the point that I even impressed some of the swearing instructors at school. But it was mighty hard to impress an eighth grader, no matter how good you were.

Inside the barn, it was warm, steamy, and comfortable. We milked by hand in those days; I milked four cows and Pa milked six. He assigned me cows that milked easiest and those with the most pleasant personalities.

With the milking finished, we carried two ten-gallon milk cans through the snow to the pump house. While we were milking, the snow had stopped and the sky had cleared. Stars twinkled everywhere. A snowstorm had raged most of the day, and the silence was near as deafening as the howling wind had been. On

33

the porch, Pa stopped to inspect the thermometer—ten below zero. The clear sky meant it would be much colder in the morning.

Inside, Ma had placed the Aladdin lamp on the kitchen table. This special kerosene lamp had a mantle and gave considerably more light than an ordinary wick lamp. Ma sat at one end of the table darning socks. A basket half full of holey socks needed her attention. She used a wooden darning egg that, thrust inside the sock, exposed the hole. She worked a crosshatch pattern across the hole, back and forth, back and forth. None of us tossed something simply because it had a hole in it. Our everyday bib overalls all bore knee patches; some of the patches had patches.

My brothers and I sat at the table working on our homework. Pa sat in a chair next to the kitchen stove, pushing in a stick of wood now and again. He was reading the day-late *Milwaukee Sentinel*. He read about the war that raged in Europe and the Pacific, and about the difficulties that rationing presented to people, especially folks living in the cities. Once or twice, he commented on how lucky we were living on a farm.

About nine, my brothers and I filed to bed, hustling up the cold stairway and along the unheated hallway. The bedroom I shared with the twins sat directly above the dining room, and the stovepipe from the dining room Round Oak heater poked through our bedroom floor, making it mostly comfortable when we crawled into bed. I slept in a single bed, while my brothers slept together in a double bed. We all wore our long underwear and socks.

We covered our heads with blankets and quilts, pretending we inhabited a submarine, deep under the North Atlantic in search of German ships. Other cold nights, my blanket would become some dark cave I'd read about at school.

The following morning, we woke to a bedroom as cold as the icehouse that stood on the Wild Rose Millpond. Below the crack that ran through one of our windows, a dusting of snow had accumulated on the interior windowsill. Frost made beautiful designs on the glass—some resembled giant ferns that twisted and turned, others looked like palm trees I'd seen in my school geography book. But we failed to appreciate the designs, instead marveling at how we could scratch off the frost with our fingers.

Pa always rose first. He started the fires in the dining room and kitchen stoves, using kerosene and kindling. I rose next to help Pa with the morning milking. By the time I had gathered my clothes and hustled through the frigid hall and down the stairs, the fire in the dining room stove was snapping and crackling. I dressed quickly by the fire, then hurried to the kitchen and pulled on my barn coat and cap. There, I grabbed my kerosene lantern off the hook, lifted the globe, and struck a match to the wick.

When I stepped outside, the air struck my face like a hunk of ice. There was no wind; the air itself was sharp and freezing. I followed Pa's tracks through the drifted snow. When the milking was finished, my brothers and I would have the chore of shoveling paths from the farmhouse to the barn, from the barn to the pump house, from the pump house to the farmhouse, from the barn to the granary, from the granary to the chicken house, and from the chicken house to the farmhouse. The buildings formed a rough circle around what we called the dooryard.

The barn was warm and rich with cow smells—clearly the warmest place on the farm these frigid winter mornings. Pa already sat milking when I arrived. I hung my kerosene lantern on a nail back of the cows, grabbed a milk pail and stool, and slid under a Holstein, embedding my head in her warm flank.

"Thirty-five below," Pa said. "Coldest morning so far this winter."

"About froze running out here," I said.

Four barn cats waited at the cat dish for Pa to pour them a little milk; they lived in odd corners of the barn and made themselves invisible except at milking time when they appeared for a handout. One was black with white feet, another was yellow, the third calico, and the fourth as gray as a foggy night.

Two streams of milk zinged against the bottom of my shiny milk pail; soon a layer of milk covered the bottom of the pail. Foam formed in the pail as I continued milking, alternating between one hand and the other. When the front two teats were milked out, I switched to the back two. The pail was about half full. In a few minutes, the back two teats were milked out as well. The rich smell of milk wafted up as I carried the nearly full pail to the milk can back of the cows. A large metal strainer sat in the can's open top, into which I slowly poured the milk. A cloth pad strained out any dust, straw, hay, or other debris.

Although tedious, hand milking had its advantages. One was the cows warmed you up, no matter how cold the morning. Milking was also a time to think. The repetition—squeeze and release, squeeze and release—had a mesmerizing effect. I thought about school. I thought about the neighbor kids. I thought about spring. I thought about summer vacation. I thought about high school and what I would do when I graduated.

Milking put you in the closest possible relationship to an animal, even closer than riding a horse. You heard the animal chewing her cud and smelled her many smells, ranging from sweet to pungent. You learned her personality, what she liked and didn't like. You found out quickly how hard to squeeze her teats to get a steady stream—not so hard as to irritate her, but hard enough to make the milk flow easily. You learned that she had good days and bad days. Some mornings she seemed genuinely pleased to see you; other mornings you were an annoyance.

Milking also allowed me to have Pa to myself. If I wanted to talk with him about something, ask him some question, this was the time. He usually milked a cow right next to mine, and the barn was quiet apart from the cows rattling their stanchions. So conversation was easy. But Pa was not the one to bring something up. He milked without saying a word, unless I spoke first.

This morning, I asked about the cold weather and the drifted roads and when he thought the snowplow would make it through and when the milkman and the mailman would come.

"Might be today," he answered. "Might be tomorrow. Might not be for several days."

The county snowplows, headquartered in the county seat of Wautoma, were huge four-wheel-drive trucks with diesel engines. Their mammoth "V" plows with wings pushed the snow to the sides of the road. They plowed the state roads first, the county roads next, and the country roads last. A week could pass before we were plowed out.

With the milking finished, we carried the milk to the pump-house, one of two other buildings where Pa kept a fire going. The pump-house stove prevented the pump from freezing. The other stove warmed the potato cellar, where we stored the fall potato crop while waiting for the prices to rise. Until we bagged the potatoes and hauled them to the potato warehouse, Pa kept the stove going, especially on below-zero days.

Pa and I returned to the house, where Ma had a stack of buckwheat pancakes waiting. My brothers, dressed and ready for school, and I took our places at the kitchen table. Just like the Holsteins had their own stalls, we each had our place at the table: Pa at one end, Ma on one side next to Duck because he was a fussy eater, Murf on the other side, and I on the end opposite Pa. We piled flapjacks on our plates and smeared them with melted lard and sorghum. These butter and sugar substitutes reminded each of us that as World War II continued in Europe and the Pacific, it affected all of us, no matter our age or where we lived.

After breakfast, my brothers and I shoveled snow, then headed for school, walking on top of the snowdrifts that blocked our unplowed road. Country school never closed, no matter how much snow fell. That was okay—I knew today I would impress the eighth graders behind the outhouse.

⌒

CHAPTER 7

Running Water

Water tank—$10.50
Barn drinking cups—$35.66
Force pump—$20.50

Our cattle and horses drank from a stock watering tank in the barnyard. Winter mornings after milking, Pa turned the animals out of their stalls. They filed out of the warm barn and shivered outside in the cold, waiting their turn at the tank.

The tank, connected to the pump house by a water pipe, was heated by a sheet-metal stove that sat immersed in the water on the bottom of the tank. Protruding above the waterline were the small stovepipe and a tube through which Pa lit the fire.

Pa ignited the fire by opening the metal door on the end of the tube, stuffing a handful of dry corn cobs down its throat, splashing in a little kerosene, and dropping in a match. With a puff and a flash, the stove burst to life. Soon the ice melted and the tank could serve its thirsty customers. A thin thread of gray smoke drifted across the snow-packed barnyard. Of course, the colder the night, the thicker the ice on the tank, the longer the ice took to melt, and the later in the morning Pa could turn the animals out.

This everyday event went on for years, from mid-November until March or even April, until one day Pa heard that Sears,

Roebuck and Co. offered a new kind of pump. This special pump forced water *up* a pipe. This meant we could run pipe wherever we wanted to, including the hayloft above the cows. If we put a water tank up there, then water—gravity fed—could be available inside the barn. Twenty years would pass before my family had running water in the farmhouse, but now the cows would get personalized drinking cups in their stalls. They would be able to drink whenever they wanted and would no longer have to huddle around the outside stock tank with its scarcely above-freezing water.

The Sears installation crew spent several days installing the new pump in the pump house. We also ran a two-inch iron pipe through the pump house roof and all the way to the barn. Pa used several discarded telephone poles to support the expanse of pipe. With considerable shoving and swearing, the Sears crew managed to lift a new water tank into the hayloft and connect it to the pipe.

In the pump house, the same gasoline engine that had driven our old pump powered the new one. But now, when we turned a couple valves, the pump would force water up the pipe and the entire distance to the hayloft. You would know when the tank was full because water ran from the overflow pipe into the barnyard.

The day arrived when everything was in order. Pa screwed tight a couple valves, opened another one, and water began pouring into the hayloft water tank. This was the big test, as Pa did not start a fire in the barnyard tank stove and did not plan to turn the cattle outside.

The cows grew restless and thirsty. A couple bellered out their unhappiness. Metal drinking cups now hung in each stall, but to get water, the cow had to push her nose down on a metal flap that allowed water to flow into her cup. Pa and I worked our way down the aisle in front of the cows, pushing down each flap and filling the cups with water. Soon several cows caught on and began pushing down the flaps themselves. All except the cow named Nancy. Either she played dumb or she was dumb, but she wanted nothing to do with anything different from what she was accustomed to. She drank only when one of us pushed the flap for her. When she had emptied her cup, she let out a mournful "moo" and we pushed the flap again.

Pa made his first mistake with the new watering system when he didn't pay attention to how long the water took to fill the hayloft tank. I glanced out the window that afternoon to see water pouring out the overflow pipe and a sheet of ice freezing over the barnyard. I hurried to the pump house and turned off the pump.

Pa's second mistake was leaving Nancy alone with her new, private watering system. Pa figured she'd simply moo all night and that would be the first thing we heard when we entered the barn the following morning.

But when Pa pulled open the barn door, everything was quiet. The problem wasn't what we heard but what we saw. Water filled the gutter back of the cows. Water filled the manger in front of the cows. Several cows stood in water. Water was everywhere.

Immediately, he suspected the hayloft tank had a loose connection. It didn't. He next suspected a water valve left open. None were.

He slopped along the manger, seeing nothing unusual—until he came to Nancy's stall. Water filled her drinking cup to the brim.

What had happened, Pa surmised, was Nancy simply held the flap down and let the water run. Her idea of a dirty trick. Her way of letting us know she wanted nothing to do with new technology. Pa and I spent more than an hour shoveling water out of the manger and then out of the gutter. It was a messy, dirty job. From that day on, Pa wedged a stone under the flap of Nancy's cup whenever he left the barn. Every morning and every evening, he removed the stone so she could drink.

The rest of the cows learned to adjust to the drinking cups. We learned a lesson, too. Just like some people, some animals have difficulty adjusting to change. And they have interesting ways of expressing their unhappiness.

CHAPTER 8

~

Hoeing

Hoe—$1.15

Come a rainy June night and, the following day too wet for making hay, Pa would say, "Guess we'd better shoulder our hoes." My brothers and I dreaded those words, because hoeing was the most boring, most uninteresting, most time-wasting job imaginable, especially when you were twelve years old.

Everyone knew hoeing was women's work. Men did manly jobs like cultivating corn and hauling hay. Ma hoed the vegetable garden out back of the house. But Pa, my brothers, and I hoed the two acres of potatoes and one acre of cucumbers. Which crops we hoed didn't matter—they were equal when it came to hoeing difficulty, if there was such a thing as degrees of hoeing difficulty.

To survive hoeing, you either had to make your mind go blank or imagine exotic things. You also had to keep one eye on Pa as you moved down a row chopping out weeds. If you slipped and chopped off a potato plant, he wouldn't say anything. But do it a second time and you were in trouble.

A two-acre potato patch didn't look like much compared to a twenty-acre hayfield. But when you were hoeing, two acres was immense. The sun baked your hide, sweat ran down your back

42

and collected around your middle, and more sweat streamed down your forehead and pooled in your eyes. You tried to ignore these discomforts as you worked on those mind-clearing or exotic thoughts. Just when you had it down—the clear mind, for instance—Pa piped up with a question.

"You know the difference between a pigweed and ragweed?"

"Huh?"

"You goin' deaf? What's the difference between pigweed and ragweed?"

I wanted to say I didn't much care about telling one weed from another. I thought I was doing good when I could tell potato plants from weeds.

"No, I don't," I answered. So much for a clear mind. Now I sensed the hot sun on my back and the rivers of sweat running over me, and I had to think besides.

Pa launched into a detailed discussion of pigweed and ragweed. He told me what they looked like when they were small, what they looked like when they were bigger, and how tall they grew if you missed one with your hoe.

My brothers, hoeing nearby, smirked while I got an advanced lesson on weeds, but they kept their hoes moving.

As long as Pa was so talkative, I decided to ask him about something else—something in the exotic-thinking category. I tried to figure out how to introduce the topic as I kept the hoe moving, digging out ragweed, pigweed, quack grass, purslane, even some thistles in the hollows.

"I've been wondering about bulls and cows," I finally said.

"What about bulls and cows?"

I hesitated, took off my straw hat, and swiped a red handkerchief across my sweaty head, then ran the handkerchief around the inside of my hat—something I'd seen Pa do often.

"I was wondering how they know to get together—how they know to breed?"

A slow smile spread over Pa's face. "Oh, they just do. It's natural."

I wanted to ask about boar and sow pigs, about billy and nanny goats, about stallions and mares, about roosters and hens—the whole lot. But I didn't. I just kept on hoeing, and thinking about Pa's answer and wondering if that's how it worked with people, too.

Several minutes passed as we hoed in silence and I thought my exotic thoughts. I glanced up at the sun to figure out the time— we had at least another hour before noon.

Instantly, my mind filled with pictures of mashed potatoes, canned beef, fresh lettuce, and strawberries. It's surprising how fast hunger replaces everything else a twelve-year-old boy has on his mind when he's hoeing.

·✑

CHAPTER 9

Town Night

One sack of flour—$1.69
Groceries from Mercantile—$2.09

Town night started with a bath in the big galvanized washtub in front of the kitchen cookstove. After six days of hard work, it was finally Saturday night and time to prepare for a drive into town so Ma could do her trading. That's what she called grocery shopping. She crated up the chicken eggs she'd collected during the week, brought them to the Wild Rose Mercantile, and traded them for groceries.

The washtub normally hung on a hook in the woodshed. No matter how dusty or hot we got the rest of the week, all we washed those days were our faces and hands. The rest we washed on bath night. Ma insisted we use Lifebuoy soap, a pinkish-red bar soap with a distinctive, medicinal smell touted in advertisements as "germ-killing." You could always tell who had bathed Saturday night because the Lifebuoy smell hung around at least a day.

In the winter, Pa brought the washtub in from the woodshed before supper so it would have a chance to warm up. Then we bathed in front of the stove, with the oven door open to add a little more warmth to the experience. The bathwater came from the reservoir attached to the cookstove. We took turns in the washtub, and although Ma added some warm water along the way, the last person bathed in essentially the same water as the first person.

Town night was a hurry-up affair. Pa and I tried to finish milking before seven o'clock, which would give us a half hour to bathe, put on clean clothes (the ones we would wear all the next week), and pile into the Plymouth with the twins, Ma, and a crate of eggs. In town, Pa parked the car in front of the Mercantile and carried the crate of eggs into the store for Ma. She and my brothers went about grocery shopping; later, they might walk over to Guth's Meat Market so Ma could trade some eggs for ring bologna or other specialty meat products. Meanwhile, Pa and I headed for Hotz's Hardware Store on the other end of Main Street.

No matter what season, a collection of farmers gathered in the back of Hotz's. In the winter, they sat around a big wood-burning stove; in the summer, they gathered near the screened backdoor, which let in a breeze and kept out the mosquitoes.

Essentially two kinds of farmers came to town on Saturday night: those who gathered in one of the town's four taverns and those who collected at Hotz's Hardware. Pa didn't have anything against drinking—especially beer, considering his strong German heritage—but the idea of sitting on a barstool never took his fancy. He never said why and I never asked. I was pleased to just sit with him in back of Hotz's, listening to the men hash and rehash the week's news and even invent some stories that never occurred.

I'd heard some of the stories before, but they got better every time. Many involved fishing and hunting and how deep the snow was twenty years ago and how it had never been so cold as when these guys were kids. Occasional exaggerations were to be expected. No storyteller wanted to bore his listeners, and sometimes the difference between a good story and a dull one was a little enhancement, a modicum of truth-stretching. Some of the men earned reputations for being "windy," and one guy was simply dubbed "liar." But nobody ever said that to his face, of course.

I couldn't tell the truth from the fiction, and I didn't much care as the stories flew and the laughter grew louder.

"Did you hear about Emil Jorgensen's pigs?"

"Nope. What about his pigs?"

"They all got out."

"How'd they manage that?"

"Snow was so hard and deep they just walked right over the fences. Hog'll do that, you know. Hogs are smart. Always looking for a way out."

"You don't say."

"I do say. You outta go out to Emil's place. I don't think he's found all his pigs yet."

Then the subject would change and somebody would tell about the time he hooked a twenty-pound northern pike while ice fishing, and when he pulled up the line, the hook had been straightened out.

"How'd you know it weighed twenty pounds if it's still in the lake?"

"At least twenty pounds. Ever try to straighten out a big fish hook? Takes at least twenty pounds of pulling. Fish might have weighed thirty pounds, probably did weigh thirty pounds."

"How'd you know you had on a fish? You mighta caught a snag, and you straightened out the hook yourself when you pulled in the line."

I knew it was time to head out when Pa snatched his watch from his pocket. He'd study it for an instant, then announce, "Well, Jerry, time to go. Your ma and brothers will be waiting for us at the Merc."

We walked back to the Mercantile, gathered up the egg crate now filled with groceries, and crawled into the Plymouth.

"Anybody for some ice cream?" Pa would say.

We cheered our approval. Who would say no to ice cream?

Pa steered the Plymouth the couple blocks to Stevens' Drugstore and parked in front. We waited in the car while he entered the brightly lit store. Soon, Pa emerged with a half-gallon of ice cream wrapped in newspaper.

When we arrived home, Ma set out some plates, while Pa pulled the butcher knife from the knife drawer and sliced the ice cream into five wedges. Nothing ever tasted better. Because our farm had no electricity, ice cream was a rare treat. Our only cooling appliance, an ice box, was nowhere near cold enough to keep ice cream from melting.

Town night ended with a bit of celebration around the kitchen table, yellow lamplight illuminating three tired boys back from a night on the town with their parents. Beyond morning and afternoon chores, Sunday would be a day of rest, usually, but not always, beginning with church. The cycle repeated, week after week.

HOMEMADE ICE CREAM

Once in a while during the winter, when plenty of ice and snow was available, Pa would suggest we make ice cream at home. Here is the recipe Ma used:

Start with one quart of cream, one cup of granulated sugar, and two teaspoons of vanilla. Watkins vanilla works best. Pour half the cream and all the sugar into a double boiler and place over the fire. Stir until the sugar is dissolved and the cream is hot. Cool and add the remaining cream and the vanilla.

Place the dasher in the center of the ice-cream can and pour in the prepared cream mixture. Replace the cover and gear frame. Fill the space around the can in the tub with shaved ice or tightly packed snow and salt. When using ice, figure about one-third salt to about two-thirds ice. With snow, figure about one-fifth salt and four-fifths snow. Pile the ice or snow over the top of the can, and begin turning the handle steadily, but not rapidly.

When you can hardly turn the handle anymore, the ice cream is frozen. Remove the dasher and put back the cover with a cork in the dasher hole. Drain the can, repack with shaved ice or packed snow, and cover with a piece of burlap or other cloth and allow standing for two hours.

While we were waiting, my brothers and I ate the ice cream on the dasher. Storebought ice cream was good, but it couldn't hold a candle to the ice cream Ma made at home.

CHAPTER 10

~

Funny Papers

Income: six dozen eggs—$2.10

Pa didn't subscribe to the Sunday paper. He figured the daily *Milwaukee Sentinel* provided us with more news than we needed, even though it came to our mailbox a day late and what we read was history rather than up-to-date material. My brothers and I didn't know about Sunday comics—what we called funny papers—until after my grandfather and grandmother Witt died.

George and Mabel Reinkert were good friends of my grandparents. The Reinkerts came from Chicago for two weeks every summer and stayed with my grandparents on the farm. During the rest of the year, Grandma mailed a crate of eggs to the Reinkerts about once a month.

After my grandparents passed away, both in 1941, Ma took over the responsibility of mailing eggs to Chicago. The egg crate—a brown, wooden, slatted box—held six-dozen eggs. Ma washed each egg, then placed them in the gray cardboard dividers that kept the eggs from touching each other. The word "Fragile" was stamped on top of the crate in big red letters. I never heard from the Reinkerts how many eggs, if any, arrived broken.

My brothers and I didn't pay any mind when Ma readied the eggs for shipping. But we sure paid attention when she received the crate back from the Reinkerts. We awaited the crate's return with nearly as much anticipation as we awaited the new Sears, Roebuck and Co. catalog.

"Egg crate come today?" I'd ask when we arrived home from school.

"Not today," Ma would answer with a smile, knowing full well why we were so interested in a plain old empty egg crate.

Because the crate wasn't empty. Mabel Reinkert had stuffed it full of Sunday comics from the *Chicago Tribune*. This was the first time we learned that Sunday papers printed colored comics, just like the comic books—or "funny books"—we infrequently got hold of at school. (We would barter at school, trading a piece of Ma's prized chocolate cake for another kid's tattered, worn-out comic book with limp pages and runny color.)

The egg crate usually arrived in the middle of a school day. Ma would sit it on a chair by the kitchen stove so we'd spot it as soon as we burst into the house. She never opened it, but left that to us.

Opening that egg crate from Chicago felt like opening a birthday present. We'd slide the wooden cover off the crate and sit it aside, exposing a huge pile of funny papers, four to six Sundays' worth. We'd sort the comics in order, wrangling over who got to read which first. The good ones continued from week to week. With the sorting finished, I turned to my favorites—*The Phantom, Superman, Jungle Jim, Joe Palooka,* and *Dick Tracy*—in each case trying to recall what grave difficulty faced them when I had last read the strip.

Reading the funny papers was like listening to our favorite radio programs each afternoon—*Captain Midnight, Terry & the Pirates,* and all the rest. These fictional characters in the comics and on the radio took me to exotic places in the world. They brought me along with them, to be a part of their adventures. They were my heroes. These men and women never gave up, no matter how tough the situation, no matter what difficulties they faced. I knew they would come through, but how would they do it? What skill would it take? Could I be like them? I would try.

With the Sunday comics, we received a big dose of adventure all at one time. The problem was that just as we got into a story, we ran out of Sundays and had to wait another month to catch up.

The day the egg crate arrived meant a painful day for getting the chores done. My brothers and I invented all sorts of excuses as to why the chores could wait. But the chores needed to be done, and Ma made sure there was no waiting. Sometimes, she even threatened to write Mabel Reinkert and tell her to keep her funny papers in Chicago. We knew Ma would never do that, but the threat remained.

After my favorites, I read *Barney Google and Snuffy Smith, Li'l Abner* and *Orphan Annie, Popeye* and *Mandrake the Magician.* Then it was over. By bedtime, we had read them all. Every page. Every colorful comic strip.

The next morning, the rumpled funny papers sat in a pile next to the kitchen wood box. Pa used the papers for starting the kitchen stove fire. The stories remained in our heads—jungle adventures, the mystery of magic, good overcoming evil.

I never forgot Mabel Reinkert's wonderful gesture. She and George had no children, but she knew what kids liked, especially farm kids who never saw a Sunday paper. Many years later, I told her how we had appreciated what she had done. She just smiled and said, "We like fresh eggs."

CHAPTER 11

~

Milking Machine

Milking machine—$225.42
Labor for installing—$6.00

"Don't ever want a milking machine," Pa said. "Hard on the cows; nothin' gentle about them machines. Heard they don't get all the milk either. Nope, don't ever want one."

Pa avidly read *Farm Journal*, *Holstein World*, and *Successful Farming*, so he knew about mechanical milking machines, how they worked, and what they cost. I figured that even if we wanted one, we'd never get one as long as we didn't have electricity. Electricity on our farm seemed a long way off.

I trudged to the barn each morning and night, milked my three cows, sometimes four, and accepted the work as one of my chores. The task wasn't altogether unpleasant, especially on cold winter mornings. Milking was at its worst on a rainy day when the cows came in from the barnyard dripping wet and reeking of damp cowhide. Rainwater trickling off a smelly cow and down your neck ranks high on the miserable scale. The most wretched thing occurred in winter, though, when the cows slept in their stalls and their wiry tails spent the night in the manure gutter. You would be innocently milking, when suddenly a manure-laden missile whopped you across the face. Compared to that, all other misery took second place.

53

Just when I thought I had Pa figured out, he'd do something I least expected. One evening at the supper table, he announced, "Bought a milking machine today. Got it at Sears and Roebuck in Berlin. They're bringin' it out later this week."

I was flabbergasted but excited, too. Pa went on to explain that electricity wasn't necessary to operate the milking machine. It would run on a Briggs & Stratton engine.

Later that week, a couple of men from Sears spent most of a day installing vacuum pipes above the cows and building a platform on one end of the barn for the vacuum pump and engine. That evening, Pa and I went out to the barn as usual come milking time, Fanny trotting behind us. But we each carried a milking machine bucket instead of an ordinary milk pail. Fastened to the bucket's sealed lid were several rubber hoses and four shiny teat cups. The fancy bucket told you right away that a milking machine differed from hand milking in that it attached to all four teats at the same time.

Inside the barn, Pa headed for the new engine. Following the instructions from the installers, he wrapped a thin rope around the engine's starting wheel and gave a mighty tug. Nothing. He adjusted the choke lever and repeated the operation. Nothing. Once more he yanked on the starting rope.

The engine fired and a roar filled the barn. The barn cats scattered. Fanny trotted to the far end of the barn and lay down nervously on a pile of straw. Even though the engine exhaust was piped outside the barn, the noise inside the barn was at a level never heard before. The vacuum pump began building a vacuum in the pipes above the stalls. The cows rattled their stanchions and relieved themselves. A cow will do that when she becomes the least bit excited. One of the first things you learn in taking care of cows is never walk behind one when she is agitated.

Pa grabbed one of the new milk pails and sat it down between two cows. He attached the rubber hose to a spigot on the vacuum line, turned the valve, and the pail came to life.

"So far, so good," Pa said. He pushed his barn cap back and began to attach the teat cups to the cow named Emily. The big Holstein craned her neck back to see what Pa was doing, likely deciding if she would allow him to keep doing it. She shuffled her feet back and forth—not a good sign.

"Easy old girl," Pa said soothingly.

Soon, the teat cups were in place. Milk flowed into the pail as Pa and I stood watching—not working, not pulling teats, not being slapped in the face with a dirty cow tail, but watching the machine work. Pa smiled. I smiled.

But Emily decided enough was enough. With a mighty swipe of one big back leg, she sent the milking machine and its tangle of rubber hoses and teat cups bouncing across the gutter. The shiny milk pail landed in cow manure.

Sometimes Pa could be very patient.

"Guess Emily is a little upset," he said. "I'll finish milking her by hand and we'll try her again tomorrow." I suspect Pa's patience stemmed from the $225.42 he had invested in the machine. I suspect it also had to do with saving face. He was not about to ask Sears to come take back its milking machine.

After a week or so of trial and error, unhappy cows, and dirtied milk pails, the cows settled down and accepted their fate. With everything running smoothly; the machine could milk three or four times as fast as we could by hand, and soon Pa had a few more cows in the milking lineup and a few more dollars in the twice-a-month milk check.

But the machines couldn't do all the work. As Pa's farm magazines foretold, the machine didn't get out all the milk. "Butterfat in those last few squirts," Pa said. "Cream always rises to the top, you know." Payment for our milk was based on its butterfat content. We had to follow the machine and "strip," or milk out, what the machine missed. From some cows, it might be only a few squirts. But other cows never grew completely comfortable with the machine, and from them we might strip out a quart or more.

The coming of the milking machine also brought an end to our once quiet, peaceful milking time. Whereas the barn atmosphere once invited easy conversation, now I had to raise my voice to be heard. With the milking machine operating, I asked only the necessary questions because unless Pa was standing near me, he couldn't hear me and I couldn't hear him. The constant whir of the engine and whoosh of the vacuum also overshadowed the subtle sounds of cattle eating, stanchions rattling, and barn cats meowing for handouts. The cats, ever adaptable, returned after the first day and gathered around their drinking dish as usual. But Fanny, who had once joined us for milking twice daily without fail, never learned to tolerate the noise and stopped accompanying us to the barn altogether.

I never regretted that Pa bought a milking machine. It made milking easier and added needed money to the milk check. But I have fond memories of the days before the milking machine, when Pa and I milked cows by hand. I remember the warmth of a Holstein's flank on a cold winter morning, when I slid under her to fill my milk pail with sweet steaming milk, foam covering the surface. I remember squirting a stream of milk toward a barn cat that sat waiting, mouth at the ready. I remember the quiet conversations with Pa, when we talked about everything from what I planned to do with my life to whether he thought it would snow that day. With the coming of a milking machine, these experiences became memories.

CHAPTER 12

The War Ends

Red Cross donation—$2.00

August 14, 1945, began as another day on the farm. I had just turned eleven and Pa considered me big enough and strong enough to help with most farm jobs. Because it was a Tuesday, I looked forward to the evening. Every Tuesday night in the summer, Wild Rose showed a free open-air movie on Main Street. Our family rarely missed a showing, from when the films started in May to the last show in early September.

The "theater" sat on a hill that gently sloped to the mill-pond. Atop the hill, the projectionist set up his green trailer, its tires blocked with chunks of split oak wood. The trailer moved from village to village throughout the summer. At the bottom of the hill, on the millpond bank, a frame held up sewed-together white sheets that served as the movie screen. The moviegoers sat on hard benches made from rough-sawed oak planks nailed to cedar posts.

Pa and I finished the barn chores and turned the cattle out to pasture by seven-thirty, giving us ample time to wash up and travel the four miles to Wild Rose. By the time we arrived, people were already filling the seats in anticipation. Many munched on popcorn purchased from the popcorn machine in front of Stevens' Drugstore. The projectionist lined up his machine and turned on the powerful light. Several of us boys made finger shadow figures on the screen.

Then I heard it—a piercing sound coming from down Main Street. *Ka-Pow, Ka-Pow.* It sounded like Pa's deer rifle.

I slid off the bench and raced up the hill. Around me, everyone left their seats and joined the throng that was gathering on both sides of Main Street. I lost track of Ma, Pa, and my brothers, but I knew they were somewhere in the crowd. A hundred yards down the street, men in uniform marched toward us. I recognized them as the Wild Rose American Legion Troop, maybe a dozen veterans dressed in their World War I uniforms. They stopped every few feet to fire their rifles into the air. With each discharge, bursts of fire shot from the rifle barrels. The smell of burnt gunpowder drifted down Main Street, mixing with the smell of popcorn.

"The war is over!" one of the men yelled. "We just got word. Japan has surrendered. It's V-J Day!"

They shot their rifles once more, and a great cheer went up from the crowd. I cheered, too. It was a happy day for everyone, almost everyone. Tears streamed down the faces of women and men—tears of joy, but also tears of sorrow. Several Wild Rose boys had died in the war. The name of every Wild Rose soldier appeared in large letters on a huge sign in front of Village Hall. A gold star was painted in front of the names of those who would not return. The same gold star hung on flags in the windows of their mothers' and wives' homes.

Down the hill, the movie came on, but almost no one watched it. Folks continued to cheer and yell, pouring in and out of the Main Street taverns, whooping and hollering and hugging each other, and kissing and waving their arms like crazy people. I watched and yelled for an hour or so. Then I felt a firm hand on my elbow.

"Come along, Jerry," Pa said. "It's time to go home." Earlier, I had seen Pa cheering with the rest, but now he was back to his quiet self, no doubt thinking about all the hard times associated with the war, and about how things would be different with no more rationing, and of the boys that would not be coming back to Wild Rose from the fighting.

The interior of the Plymouth was quiet as we made our way along County Highway A, then turned north on the dirt road that ran by our farm. We had talked about the war in school nearly every day, and Ma donated a small portion of our precious farm income to the international Red Cross to help with wartime relief. I thought about the men I knew who had gone off to fight, many of them relatives.

My uncles would tell us where my cousins were stationed and what battles they had fought in. And we occasionally received a V-mail from my cousin Kermit. The letters, sent from his base in England, showed up with holes where they had been censored.

Even with all the uncertainties and inconveniences, we had continued living our lives. I often imagined what it would be like to see German soldiers come marching up our dirt road, or German tanks—like the ones pictured in *The Weekly Reader* at school—rolling up Highway 51. I had my .22 rifle, and Pa had his 30-30 Savage deer rifle, his .22, plus a huge, old, double-barreled shotgun. I figured we were in pretty good shape if those Germans wanted to take over central Wisconsin. It wouldn't be easy for them.

Sometimes, my brothers and I would play war, a sort of practice for if the Germans did come. Except nobody wanted to be a German soldier. Nobody wanted to be the bad guy. With all good guys, our war games generally fizzled before they started. Without two sides, there isn't much of a war, even a play war.

Ma spoke and read German; her grandparents had come from Germany. So had Grandmother Apps. Many of the folks in our community were German—the Millers, the Handrichs—so people were torn about the war. There was no question about loyalty to America and distaste for Hitler. But families worried about relatives still living in Germany and whether cousins would end up fighting cousins.

My friend Jim Kolka, just six months younger than me, lived on a farm about a mile west of our place. His mother had come to this country from Czechoslovakia. "Mail doesn't get through to my folks anymore," Mrs. Frank Kolka said. "Don't even know if they're still alive." Jim was my best friend. I wanted to tell him how sorry I was about his grandparents, but I didn't know how to say it without sounding sappy, so I never said anything.

Pa turned the Plymouth into our driveway. I finally broke the silence and asked, "Will we be able to buy sugar now?"

Ma laughed. "I hope so," she said. "I sure hope so."

⌐

CHAPTER 13

New Barn

Barn— $500.00
Cost to move barn—$350.00
New stanchions (8)—$28.20

"Not much of a barn," Pa said, especially during haying season. Our barn's second-story hayloft was too small to accommodate a mechanized hayfork, which meant we had to pitch hay into the hayloft by hand. This job usually fell to me. I would climb to the top of the hay wagon and pitch hay through two large hay doors on the barn's west side. This wasn't such a tough job from the top of the hay load, but with each forkful, the job grew more difficult. By the time I got near the bottom of the load, I was pitching hay as high as I could toss it. Hay leaves filtered down my neck, sticking to my sweaty back, and my arms ached more with each forkful.

Pa worked inside the barn. He carried the hay from the doorway to the far corners of the hayloft, stacking it until scarcely enough room remained to stand and his pitchfork handle banged against the roof.

As dairy barns go, ours was not only small but poorly constructed. It had a gable roof design but was framed with two-by-sixes and two-by-fours rather than ten-by-ten timbers and posts. The barn was about thirty-eight feet long and maybe twenty-four feet wide. It was of all wood construction from top to bottom, two stories high, but not near as tall or roomy as the timber barns built during this era. Windstorms frequently boiled up from the west, taking a toll on the insufficient framing and causing the entire barn to lean to the east.

I knew Pa wanted a bigger, better barn. Scarcely a day went by that he didn't grumble about it, but building materials and carpenters were in short supply during the war years. Lumber was both hard to get and expensive, and building a new barn would have cost several thousand dollars. Besides, many young carpenters were off fighting in the war or working at higher-paying jobs in city factories making military equipment. "Guess we gotta put up with it for a while yet," Pa said.

Then Pa bought the milking machine and his desire for a new barn intensified. He wanted to expand our dairy herd, but our barn would accommodate only the ten we already milked, especially when space was necessary to shelter three horses, a herd bull, and several calves.

Finally, in spring 1946, Pa found a solution to his problem. It came in the form of a previously built barn, located about four miles away on a small farm. The owner had gone out of dairy farming and no longer needed the structure. Constructed with huge timbers, the barn had enough space in the hayloft so you could pull in a wagonload of hay and unload it with a mechanical hayfork. Pa decided to attach the new barn to the end of the old barn. The lower sections would become one, and we would have space for three times as many cattle. This second-hand barn may not have fulfilled Pa's dreams of building a brand new barn, but it was about as good a barn as he could hope for under the circumstances.

I accompanied Pa the day he closed the deal. He bought the barn for five hundred dollars and paid the farmer with five one-hundred-dollar bills. As Pa plunked down each bill, the farmer's eyes grew bigger. I suspect he had never seen so many large bills before; I know I hadn't.

Moving this huge old barn proved to be a challenge. Pa hired Neil Darling, a building mover, to oversee the operation. Neil was a tall, thin man with graying hair and a cigarette stuck in his mouth most of the time. His right hand was mostly missing; a thumb and one finger remained. I didn't ask, but he had likely smashed it in a moving project.

When Neil saw the barn, he said, "Nothin' to it." I suspect he said that about all his moving projects. Four miles of tree-studded country road lay between our barn and its new home. "Gotta get rid of all them tree limbs hangin' over the road," Neil said. "There ain't enough room to move a outhouse down these roads the way they're grown over."

For three weeks, the hired man, Pa, my brothers, and I cut branches. I had often helped Pa cut wood for the woodstoves, and this was worse. When you make wood, first you fell the tree, then you saw off the branches. Fairly straightforward. For this, we had to crawl up the trees and whack off branches in midair.

After we had chopped the last branch, Pa called Neil Darling, and the following week, the crew arrived. They moved in with us, all four of them. Pa said they could have the big bedroom upstairs, and that's where they slept. They ate their meals with us, too. For Ma, it was like feeding a small threshing crew three meals a day.

Moving a barn takes a while. The crew spent most of a week separating the barn from its foundation, jacking it up, and putting timbers under it. They took another couple days to ease Neil's huge old Diamond T moving truck under the barn, extending the bed some forty feet, and then, with rusty-looking screw jacks, slowly letting the massive barn down on the truck.

The barn was so large that Neil figured his truck alone wouldn't have enough power to tote it, especially uphill. So Pa asked our neighbor Bill Miller to bring his John Deere B tractor the day of the move, and Pa brought his Farmall H.

It was something to see. Pa hooked the H to the front of the moving truck, and Bill chained his Deere to the front of the H. If you happened to be out for a drive and saw all this coming toward you, first you'd see the Deere and hear the *pop pop* of its two-cylinder engine, then you'd spot our Farmall and see the smoke spitting from its exhaust stack and hear its engine roaring, then you'd see the big Diamond T truck and hear its roar mixing with the Farmall's, and finally you'd see the barn. Of course, then you'd have to turn around and find another route, because the barn filled the road from ditch to ditch.

The parade moved slowly down the road. I walked alongside the barn with the crew, watching for overlooked branches hanging over the road. We also tried to guide the drivers—Pa on the H, Bill on the B, and Neil in the truck—down the middle of the road, where they would encounter less problems. Occasionally, they had to stop for an overhanging limb, and everyone waited while one of the workmen shinnied up the tree and sawed off the branch.

All went well until we arrived at the railroad tracks. Here, we discovered the barn could not pass under the telegraph wires strung along the tracks. Neil walked to a nearby farm and put in a call to the Chicago Northwestern Railroad people, and then we waited. A track crew was stationed in Wild Rose, so they had but a few miles to travel to reach us. An hour passed before the workers arrived, and they were not happy with what they saw. They had hoped they could merely loosen the wires and lift them over the barn. It hadn't occurred to them that barns could be so tall.

"Can't cut these wires," the foreman said. "It'll interrupt telegraph transmission all over this part of the stare."

Neil Darling was not one to accept no. The following conversation included a lot of hand waving, pointing toward the barn, and some considerable shouting. The next thing I saw was a workman crawling up a telegraph pole and cutting the wires.

Neil motioned for the tractors and truck to cross the tracks, and
we continued on our way.

By late afternoon, the barn arrived at the farm. Overhanging
branches had pulled off a few shingles along the roof edges, but
otherwise the building appeared in fine shape. The next several
days the men spent joining the old barn to the new one, attempt-
ing to make the two barns one. A mason arrived and laid concrete
blocks to form a barn wall. A bulldozer came and pushed soil to
make a ramp leading to the haymow.

A few weeks later, the workers completed the job. The barn
was in place. The smell of freshly poured concrete temporarily
took the place of cattle smells.

That afternoon, Pa and I stood inside the new barn. He wore
a huge grin. The lower part had room for more than twenty stanchions, plus two horse stalls, a bull stall, and a substantial calf pen.
The barn also had enough open space to drive a manure spreader
inside, making manure handling easier. Silage feeding was easier,
too, because the manger extended the length of the stanchions,
making the task more convenient.

The upstairs was a thing of beauty. Wooden pegs fastened
together the huge wooden timbers. A haymow bordered each
side of the new barn's driveway—or threshing floor, as old-timers
called it—which we would use for unloading hay. Huge doors
opened onto the barn's driveway, allowing room for a wagonload
of hay. And above it all, hanging from a track that ran the length of
the barn, was a mechanical hayfork with an assortment of pulleys
and ropes. From this day forward, barn life would be different in
nearly every respect.

Pa took one last look down the row of stanchions before head-
ing to the house for supper. "Pretty good barn," he said.

CHAPTER 14

~

Electricity Arrives

Pump jack and electric motor—$62.50
Wiring buildings, Mr. Payne and Mr. Lower—$80.00
One yard light post (used telephone pole)—$2.90
Electric bill—$4.00

When I was a kid, I had pretty much accepted the idea that electricity was only for townspeople. Just two farms in our community had electric power throughout the war years. The rest of us powered our machines with gasoline engines and lighted our homes with kerosene lamps. On the home farm, my family used five kerosene lamps to illuminate the farmhouse. Two wick lamps lit the kitchen, one from the kitchen table and the other from its hook on the wall. Two more lit the upstairs bedrooms. These lamps were smaller and easier to carry than the kitchen lamps. Ma gave me my grandmother Witt's bedroom lamp when I was ten, and I proudly carried this smart little lamp up to my bedroom every night. The final lamp sat on the dining room table. This powerful Aladdin lamp emitted more than twice the light of an ordinary wick lamp.

Ma looked forward to electric lights, when she would no longer have to refill the kerosene in the kerosene lamps every week, or wash their glass chimneys. She wanted electric bulbs scattered

around her house like the ones in our grandparents' farmhouse—
one of the two neighborhood farms with electricity. They were
tiny little bulbs by today's standards, but they gave considerably
more light than our smoky kerosene lamps. Though Ma never
said so, we all knew she also wanted an electric clothes iron like
Grandmother Witt's. Ma ironed with a heavy flat iron, called a
sadiron, heated on the woodstove. Ma also wanted an electric
motor to replace the hard-to-start Briggs & Stratton gas engine
that powered her washing machine.

Pa wanted an electric motor, too, to replace the Briggs & Stratton engine that ran the milking machine. It started hard, I suspect,
because of all the moisture in the barn. Pa might pull the starter
rope for a half hour or more before the reluctant beast would take
off and we could commence milking. Pa also wanted an electric
motor to replace the gas engine that pumped water for the livestock. And he wanted electric bulbs to replace kerosene lanterns
in all the outbuildings, including the barn and the haymow.

Secretly, I wanted electricity, too. I wanted to invite my town
friends over and not be ashamed when they had to read by lamplight. I wanted to feel equal to my city cousins. I wanted a record
player and an electric erector set. If one thing made rural and
urban life different, it was electricity.

Every year, Pa paid a visit to Wisconsin Power and Light. Back
in the early 1930s, the company had strung electric lines along
our farm's northern side, connecting Wild Rose with Almond, a
town northwest of us. Pa talked to them about running a line a
quarter mile to our farm buildings.

Every year, they said no. Something about farmers not using
enough electrical power to warrant running a line.

Pa returned every year to see if their policy had changed, but
the salesmen kept saying no. Pa never said anything to us kids,
but every time he came back from a visit, he was furious. His

face was red and he said little. Plus, we overheard him telling Ma about the meeting and cussing the electric company. He cussed a lot when he was mad.

In town, folks had been hooked up to electricity since 1908, when Edward Hoaglin, the local miller, installed an electrical generator at the gristmill. Water power turned the generator, and the people of Wild Rose had electric power every evening, from dusk until eleven o'clock at night, when Hoaglin flipped a switch and turned off the power. He had to turn the electricity off so the millpond could fill and maintain a sufficient head of water to run the mill, which he used primarily to grind cattle feed for farmers.

Over the next couple decades, the villagers' electricity needs grew and soon they were using more than the mill could generate. Meanwhile, farmers had long waits for their milling because the generator was using up all the water power. Finally, in 1925, Hoaglin sold his generating equipment to Wisconsin Power and Light, which had the ability to bring in electricity from the outside. But farms still had no electricity.

The situation looked the same across the country. Towns and cities had electricity; most rural areas did not. Electric companies across the nation felt the same way about stringing lines to farms as did Wisconsin Power and Light: they didn't want to hook up farmers, they couldn't make any money from rural customers, and so on. But this was about to change. In 1935, President Franklin D. Roosevelt signed an executive order establishing the Rural Electrification Administration (REA). The following year, REA became a permanent, independent government agency that would provide loans to establish electric cooperatives in rural communities. Now, there was hope. If private electric companies wouldn't string lines to farms, federally funded electric cooperatives would.

Local farmers immediately began talking about the REA bringing electricity to our neighborhood. To accomplish this, the agency would have to establish an electric cooperative in Waushara County. But it wasn't until 1940 that Henry Hafer-becker, the county agricultural agent, finally held a general meeting to discuss organizing a cooperative. Within one year of the meeting, the Waushara County electric cooperative began operations. Workers constructed a substation and began setting poles and stringing wires. It looked like our neighborhood would finally have electricity.

But World War II put a damper on the entire operation. For the next couple years, no electricity flowed through the new lines. In 1943, a special War Production Board Order allowed food-producing farms to receive electrical service. Even then, a copper-wire shortage made full service impossible. By the war's end in 1945, the REA cooperative had hooked up only 873 farms, a small percentage of the farms in all of Waushara County, to electrical service. Our home farm was not one of them.

In spring 1946, Pa once more asked Wisconsin Power and Light if the company would run a line to our farm.

"We most certainly will," the salesman said. "How soon do you want it?"

"A little competition sure helps," Pa said that night at the supper table. "Now we've got to find somebody to wire us up."

Pa hired two electricians, Mr. Payne and Mr. Lower, to prepare our farm for electricity. Within a few days, the men began stringing wires through the farmhouse walls, placing switches near the doors, and hanging fixtures from the ceilings. They placed a used telephone pole halfway between the house and the barn and attached a yard light to it. How wonderful, I thought, to have the entire path between the house and the barn lighted. Soon, they completed the wiring in the barn. A string of light bulbs marched across the ceiling from north to south, behind the cows. The electricians installed two light bulbs covered with unbreakable glass shields in the haymow—no more dangerous kerosene lanterns there. They hung light bulbs in the chicken house, the granary and wagon shed, and the woodshed and pump house.

At suppertime one evening, Ma said, "We'll never be able to pay for that much light. Electricity is gonna send us to the poor farm."

But Pa, undaunted, found even more places for the electricians to string wires, such as the brooder house and the hog pen. "Those little chickens and little pigs sure don't need electric lights," Ma said. She had not yet learned about electric brooder stoves or heat lamps, which would save many little animals during cold spring weather.

When the electricians finished, light bulbs hung everywhere except the outhouse. Pa said if you intended to read in the outhouse—and a Sears, Roebuck and Co. catalog could usually be found on the seat—then you should visit in the daylight. At night, Pa's theory was attend to your business and leave. Besides, you could always take along a kerosene lantern. It gave off a little heat, which was welcome on cold winter nights.

Payne and Lower completed wiring the farm by late summer. But the ground froze before Wisconsin Power and Light had a chance to place the poles. My brothers and I had great fun flipping the switches on and off, imagining brilliant light flooding the rooms. Come April, crews could set poles and string wires from the main line to our farm. In the meantime, my brothers and I had the entire winter to flip switches and imagine.

For Christmas that year, I received an electric wood-burning set, the kind that burned designs in wood. As with the light switches, I could only imagine how the set worked until the power came on. My folks also gave us kids an erector set with an electric motor. Its many metal pieces could be bolted together to create everything from building cranes to farm tractors. My brothers and I built the electric motor into many of our creations, but we could only guess what it would do. Naturally, we wasted no time telling town kids about our new erector set and its electric motor. We didn't mention that it didn't work.

The winter of 1946 to 1947 was a time of great expectation. I have never looked forward to anything as much as I looked forward to electricity. By this time, our country school had electricity, so each day my brothers and I sat in a well-lighted schoolroom. We especially appreciated the school's electric motor and pump jack that pumped water with the flip of a switch. Previously, one of us older students had pumped water by hand. The task amounted to pumping the handle up and down until the water ran and filled a pail. It wasn't unpleasant, except in winter when the pump handle was freezing cold.

At home, as we had done for many winters, Pa and I carried kerosene lanterns to the barn each morning and evening. Pa rolled the wheelbarrow carrying two empty ten-gallon milk cans along the well-worn path from the pump house to the barn. His lantern swung on the wheelbarrow handle, casting eerie shadows on the barnyard fence. I carried the other lantern, usually on the run, although Pa had warned me more than once that if I tripped and dropped the lantern, I'd have to scrape up the money for a broken chimney.

In the barn, I hung my lantern on a nail behind the cows, toward the south end. Pa hung his on the north end. Somewhere in between the two lanterns, the overlap of their meager yellow light failed, creating a dark and mysterious place where cats slurped warm milk and—in my imagination—unknown creatures lurked.

Even more eerie was the haymow in winter. Each evening after milking, I unhooked my lantern from the wall and crawled up the ladder into this space above the cattle. Huge cobwebs hung everywhere. I hung the lantern off to the side, because dry hay would burn like kindling if the lantern flames ever touched it. The light cast huge shadows against the walls. In my mind, the shadows came from alien monsters, or wild animals like the Kodiak bears I read about in *Outdoor Life*, poised ready to leap on me with scarcely a growl.

My job was to pitch loose hay down to Pa, who forked it to the cows. The haymow lay directly above the cattle mangers, and I pitched the hay through two large holes in the floor. In the winter, moisture from the cattle moved upward, freezing when it collided with the haymow's colder air. Frost clung to the long, wispy cobwebs, making beautiful artistic displays. But after forking hay through the tangle of frost and cobwebs, with aliens and animals lurking in the shadows, I failed to appreciate the aesthetics of the moment.

February dragged into March, and the snow began melting. Cold, dreary, and sometimes snowy days slowly gave way to sunshine and warmer temperatures. April arrived, but still the ground hadn't thawed and the electric-company crews could not work.

Then, one day in mid-April, I arrived home from school to see a black electric post standing in front of our house. The crew had arrived and placed the four poles necessary to hook us to the main power line. It wouldn't be long now. I said that at the supper table that night and Pa was smiling and Ma was smiling and my brothers were grinning. It had been a long wait.

A few days later, the crew strung the wires, hung the transformer, and connected everything. Finally, our farm was ready for electricity. That evening, we gathered in the kitchen to watch Pa flip on the kitchen light for the first time. Above us, two long fluorescent bulbs hung on the kitchen ceiling. The kerosene lamp still sat in the center of the kitchen table. "Just in case this new-fangled stuff doesn't work," Ma said.

"Well, here goes," Pa said. He flipped the switch with an exaggerated motion, and brilliant light bathed the kitchen. We all stood blinking. Never before had the kitchen been so bright.

Ma looked around, on top of the ice box, behind the cookstove, alongside the kitchen sink.

"Oh my gosh," Ma said. "Oh my gosh."

"What's wrong?" Pa asked.

"My kitchen's dirty, so dirty. I never knew I had such a dirty kitchen. What have people thought all these years?"

"You didn't see the dirt," Pa said. "Other people didn't see the dirt either." He was never one to get excited about a little dirt here and there. Farming involved lots of dirt and dust.

Ma kept looking around and finding dust and grime she never knew existed. She began cleaning that evening, and she cleaned every day for most of the week until the kitchen was spotless, even under the glare of our new fluorescent lights.

Meanwhile, my brothers and I ran through the house, flipping switches on and off. We plugged in the elaborate crane we had made from our erector set. We watched it work. It was like magic. The little pulley on the motor turned because of this mysterious force that ran through wires. What a wonderful thing it was.

That night, when Pa and I went to the barn for the evening milking, we left our kerosene lanterns in the house. With the flip of a switch, the entire barn glowed in light. There were no corners filled with shadows. The barn cats didn't know what to make of it. Even the cows blinked with all the light.

Pa looked around the barn at the dust that had accumulated through the long winter.

"Guess we'll have to whitewash the barn as soon as it warms up a little more," Pa said. "Didn't know it was this dirty in the barn."

⁓

CHAPTER 15

County Agent

Alfalfa seed—$61.70 ($27.00 per bushel)
Medium-clover seed—$10.80 (one bushel)
Timothy seed—$3.25 (one bushel)
Lime—$8.60 (four tons)
Lime spreader—$6.00 (used)
2-12-6 fertilizer—$68.20 (two tons)

After finishing morning chores and accomplishing some farm work, Pa headed into Wild Rose for a noon meeting. The county agent, Henry Haferbecker, had set it up to talk about a new farming idea researched by the University of Wisconsin's College of Agriculture. Twenty-five or thirty farmers gathered at the American Legion Hall. Most wore bib overalls and caps with implement logos—John Deere, Allis-Chalmers, International Harvester. The Wild Rose Midland Cooperative provided a free lunch, and no farmer would pass up a free meal—or a chance to visit with fellow farmers.

At the meeting, Haferbecker talked about hay and milk production. The farmers in our region fed their livestock hay made from timothy, a grass commonly grown for hay in Wisconsin. But Haferbecker said university research showed that alfalfa had more protein and vitamins than timothy. As a result, cows fed hay made from alfalfa gave more milk. The research was clear. If you switched from timothy to alfalfa, your cows would produce more milk and your farm income would rise. At the same time, you should continue growing timothy for your horses, since they don't give milk and alfalfa hay may be too rich for them.

Now, to most farmers, hay was hay. What kind didn't matter as long as you had a lot of it. Some even fed their livestock marsh hay made from wild grasses that grew in low areas. After all, if a farmer expected his cows and horses to survive Wisconsin's long winter, he needed a full hayloft. Timothy was cheap, grew well, and you could feed it to both your horses and cows. What more could a farmer want?

From a sheer cost perspective, most farmers thought they couldn't afford to grow alfalfa. The Wild Rose Midland Cooperative sold alfalfa seed for twenty-seven dollars a bushel, compared to timothy seed at just $3.25 a bushel.

Furthermore, central Wisconsin has acres of sandy soil. Sandy soil tends to be acidic. Timothy grows well in acidic soil; alfalfa does not. Haferbecker explained that you couldn't just plant alfalfa seed and expect a crop. You had to apply lime to reduce the soil's acidity. "Lime is mostly calcium carbonate," Haferbecker said. "You can buy it for two or three dollars a ton."

The farmers at the meeting may not have known what calcium carbonate was, but they knew how to figure. They added up the cost of alfalfa seed, the cost of lime, the further cost of spreading it, and they left the meeting shaking their heads.

Henry Haferbecker worked out of an office on the third floor of the Wautoma courthouse, a space he shared with a secretary and a Home Demonstration agent who worked with rural women in the county. He was a short, round-faced man who always wore a dress shirt open at the neck, belted pants, and a felt hat. The

College of Agriculture and Waushara County jointly employed him to bring new farming research results from the university to our county. You might think farmers would grab up new ideas for doing things better. They didn't.

If your pa did something the way his pa did it, well, it would take a major shift in thinking for him to change. "If it was good enough for Pa, it's good enough for me," I heard more than one farmer say.

This attitude applied to everything from planting corn to selecting dairy cattle. Farmers changed their way of thinking mighty slowly sometimes. What a farmer liked to do was watch his neighbor. If his neighbor tried something new, and it worked for a couple years, then he might try it. *Might* try it. Some bullheaded farmers never tried anything new.

So Haferbecker, and all the other county agents working in rural areas across the nation, faced major hurdles trying to convince farmers to make some basic changes. But not every farmer turned down Haferbecker's ideas. Pa and a couple neighbors, the Macijeskis and the Swendryznskis, bought lime, spread it on their hay fields, and planted the expensive alfalfa seed. With some timely rains that summer, the alfalfa got off to a good start. Alfalfa is a perennial and doesn't really come into its own until the second or third year of planting. By the following summer, farmers were stopping on the road alongside our alfalfa field to see what was growing there. Henry Haferbecker also became a good friend of Pa's and of mine. He made an important difference in how we farmed in his quiet, unassuming, but well-informed way.

Haferbecker also helped organize 4-H clubs around the county, including one in our school district. We named it the Chain O' Lake 4-H Club and met monthly, sometimes in the homes, sometimes at the schoolhouse. Kids could sign up for a variety of projects in agriculture and home economics. Both boys and girls flocked to dairy. Most of the girls also signed up for clothing or food projects. In addition to dairy, I signed up for forestry and the field-crops projects.

I didn't think about it at the time, but doing 4-H projects not only taught us about new farming and forestry approaches, it was also a good way to convince our fathers to try new practices. For example, I read in my 4-H forestry bulletin that woodlots should be fenced to keep cattle out, so little trees would have a chance to grow. This bulletin said that for a woodlot to be sustainable, new trees must be allowed to grow and thrive. With cattle grazing off the new seedlings, only the old trees remained. I mentioned this to Pa, who had always pastured our woodlot, which meant he allowed the cows to roam around the woods eating what they might.

Although Pa had been quick to plant alfalfa, he wasn't too sure about fencing off the woodlot. After all, his pa had allowed cattle in the woods, as did most of the neighbors. Pa held out all summer, and then one day, he finally agreed to sink some new fence posts and to string barbed wire around the woodlot. For the first time, it was free of hungry cows.

For the first few years after we fenced off the woods, wild blackberry bushes appeared everywhere and we picked blackberries by the pailful. Never before had Ma made so many blackberry pies, or canned as much blackberry sauce. We'd gotten an unexpected benefit from fencing off the woods, and sooner than we thought, too.

Within five years, our woodlot changed dramatically, from an open park-like place to one of heavy undergrowth and many new trees. Over the same time period, almost every farmer in our neighborhood began growing alfalfa hay and shipping a can or two more milk from their dairy herds each day, except for one farmer who absolutely refused to change.

Haferbecker was a most patient man. He provided information, answered questions, visited farms, walked hayfields, checked on haymows, even looked at your milk records if you wanted him to. But as hard as he worked, for each idea, one farmer always held out.

"Never can trust that university," the holdout would say. "They're in cahoots with the alfalfa seed salesmen. Besides, having too much information is not a good thing—just clutters up thinking."

CHAPTER 16

❧

School Picnic

One packet Jell-O—$.10
Two packets grape Kool-Aid—$.10
One lemon—$.05

When my family arrived for the end-of-the-year school picnic, cars already lined both sides of the dusty road. The school board had set up makeshift tables alongside the white schoolhouse, under some giant black oak trees. The tables were made of the same planks and sawhorses that appeared onstage during the Christmas program. Mothers had spread tablecloths over the planks, and our teacher, Mrs. Faith Jenks, helped direct where to place the food. Fathers gathered under the oaks, enjoying a few hours away from the fieldwork that beckoned everyone this time of year. It was corn planting time. But the school picnic took precedence over farm work.

Ma had been busy all morning preparing potato salad, making a carrot Jell-O concoction, baking a chocolate cake, slicing homemade bread for bologna sandwiches, stirring up a batch of grape Kool-Aid, and slicing fresh lemon into the half-gallon jug. The teacher gave the same instructions for the picnic each year: bring a dish to pass, silverware, and sandwiches enough for your own family. Of course, Ma's sandwiches would be mixed in with the rest, so we didn't have to eat bologna if we didn't want to.

This picnic would be my last at the Chain O' Lake School. I had just finished eighth grade, the final grade at our one-room country school. Next year, I would take the bus to Wild Rose High School.

The school picnic was a highlight for all the students; it celebrated the end of the school year. The picnic was a chance for the students and the community to say thank you to the teacher. This past year, one teacher had taught fifteen students enrolled in all eight grades. The picnic was also an opportunity for the teacher to thank the students and their parents. It was a joyous event for everyone.

Parents enjoyed socializing at the picnic and other school events, but their attendance also spoke to the importance placed on education. Almost everyone in our community was a first- or second-generation immigrant from an assortment of countries— Norway, England, Wales, Poland, Russia, Germany, Czechoslovakia. They all believed in the importance of an education to get ahead. Their support for the little white school never wavered. It was clearly "their" school and remained so until the school consolidations of the mid-1950s and 1960s.

These same farmers considered schooling beyond high school another matter. "Too much schooling is not a good thing," I often heard from our neighbors and from one of Pa's brothers. "Too much learning and a kid will want to leave the farm." There was truth to his statement. Roy Handrich, one of the neighbor boys, had gone off to college right after World War II, and he never returned to farming. "He took up school teaching," said his brother Arlin, who remained on the farm. As for me, I looked forward to high school and returning to the home farm. It was what the oldest son in a family was supposed to do.

With the food in place, Mrs. Jenks announced it was time to eat, and everyone lined up on both sides of the table. We heaped our plates with potato salad, dill pickles, Jell-O, baked beans,

cake and pie, and of course sandwiches of every description—
bologna, strawberry jam, chicken salad, cheese, egg salad, and
even peanut butter, which I considered a waste of good bread.

The school board had also bought five gallons of vanilla ice
cream. It came in a couple two-and-a-half-gallon metal tubs in-
sulated in a huge canvas carrier, to prevent melting. One of the
fathers took charge of dipping, and everyone lined up for one
or more scoops. After the feast, with everyone filled to bursting,
the mothers put away the food, while the fathers sat under the
trees relaxing, smoking their pipes, and talking about cows, corn
planting, and the hay crop.

My classmates and I, however, were thinking about what was
to come. Outside of a grand meal, the school picnic featured
a softball game between the students and their fathers. Few of
the fathers had played softball since the previous year's picnic,
whereas us kids played every day. Any student who wanted to
play—boys, girls, first graders on up—could and usually did play.
So did the fathers, except those who had gimpy legs and figured
they couldn't make it around the bases.

The ritual softball game was more than a game. It was an opportunity for us to see our fathers play. We had seen our fathers
work—all the time. But on this day, we saw our fathers having
fun, throwing a softball, running around the bases, laughing and
acting like kids. The ball field filled with children of all ages, from
six-year-olds to those in their fifties.

I remember when Pa came up to bat. He took softball as seri-
ously as he took farming. I was pitching and there was Pa, picking
up a bat. He spit on his hands, like he did when he picked up an ax,
and then he hunched over the plate. He stared down at me on the
pitcher's mound—it was more a sandy hole than a mound—and,
without putting it in words, said, *Show me what you got.*

Not to be boastful, but I was a fair to middling softball pitcher.
At least, I had struck-out some of the better batters from Dopp

School, one of the country schools we played each year. I let fire
with my fastball—underhand, of course—and Pa took a mighty
swing. He missed, almost falling on his keester.

"Strike one," Mrs. Jenks, the umpire for the game, announced
loudly.

Pa's face turned red. He made ready for my second pitch.

"Hey, Herm," Bill Miller yelled. "Bat got a hole in it?"

Pa acted like he hadn't heard, but his face grew even redder.

I wound up and, this time, slipped my slowball across the outside of the plate. Pa took another mighty swing and the ball shot
straight up in the air, about as high as one of our tallest pines. Jim
Kolka, the first baseman, walked over and stood under where he
knew the ball would fall and caught it easily.

"Out," Mrs. Jenks said in her authoritative voice.

As usual, the students won the game. I don't remember the
score, but I remember what a wonderful time I had. By mid-
afternoon, it was time to go home. My family piled into the Plymouth and drove home with the leftover food. I expected to hear
something about the game from Pa. What he said, with a smile
and big twinkle in his eye, was, "You had a lucky day, Jerry. I didn't
want to show you up by hitting a home run."

In my eyes, Pa had hit a home run just by playing the game,
being a good sport, and taking his turn batting.

Then, when I walked into the house, Ma handed me a little
box.

"What's this?" I asked.

"Open it and you'll find out."

I tore off the wrapping and found a Pocket Ben watch, the
same kind that Pa carried. Pa had already wound it and set it to
the correct time.

"It's a present for finishing eighth grade," Pa said.

"Thank you," I said. I put my new watch in the pocket of my overalls. It had been a good day. I looked forward to the next four years of high school, but first came summer on the farm and all the work that entailed. I did not know then—did not have the slightest inkling—that in four years, I would be leaving the farm.

CHAPTER 17

⌐~

Making Hay

Baling hay—$20.00

Our neighbor John Swendryznski bought the first hay baler in our
community. The machine, a J. I. Case wire-tie baler, took three
fellows to operate: one on the tractor and two on the baler. The
two on the baler sat on little seats toward the back, facing each
other, while a hay bale formed between them. One man pushed
a two-pronged steel needle through the packed hay, then fed two
hanks of hay wire along each prong, one on top and one on the
bottom. The fellow on the other side caught the two pieces of
wire and hooked them together. Usually a kid did the tying, as
the process was called. Both jobs required people who could take
a considerable amount of dust. Earth and hay leaves boiled up as
the baler moved around the field. The roar of the big Wisconsin
gasoline engine and the *thump, thump* of the baler plunger were
always in the background.

Stationary hay balers had been invented in the late 1800s but
were seldom used because no one wanted to haul their hay to the
baler. Before Swendryznski bought his portable hay baler, our
family made hay the same way farmers had for several hundred
years. In mid-June, Pa would hitch our draft horses to the old

McCormick five-foot sickle bar mower and head out to the hay field. Around and around the field the machine clattered on its steel wheels. Fresh hay, sometimes three feet tall, toppled to the ground to dry in the sun.

If the day was warm, with bright sunshine and a southern breeze, and the crop not too tall or too rank, the hay would be ready for raking and bunching by late afternoon. Pa hitched the team to a high-wheeled dump rake with half-moon iron tines some four feet high. Compared to the sickle bar mower, it pulled easy. Pulling the rake, the team walked briskly around the field, forming the hay into long rows.

While Pa drove the team, my brothers and I were usually stuck hoeing potatoes, beans, or cucumbers, or perhaps helping Ma pick strawberries. Once the hay had been raked, we knew what came next. We forked the hay into round bunches about four feet high. Bunching hay helped it dry and protected the crop in case of an unexpected rain shower.

Bunching hay was not quite as boring as hoeing. We never finished hoeing. Bunching hay had a visible end, though some of our hayfields extended twenty acres, and the piles of raked hay seemed to go on forever. Start at the end of a raked row, use your three-tine fork to push the hay into a neat pile—it had better be neat because if it tipped over, Pa would let you know—top it off with a sizable forkful, and move to the next bunch. One bunch after the other until dozens of them lay behind you, dozens and dozens, and you didn't want to see another one, ever. But you did. You couldn't cheat when bunching hay. You either made a hay bunch or you didn't. When you hoed, you could slack off, move a little more slowly, even skip a weed or two—though you'd best not be caught.

After Pa finished raking, he tied up the team and helped us. Pa made bunching hay look easy. His work had a rhythm, free-flowing and easy, no effort wasted. He could make two bunches

for every one I made, and he seemed to enjoy every minute of
the process.

When bunching hay, every bit of effort, or lack of effort, was
visible. The best part—outside of that wonderful smell of drying alfalfa, timothy, and clover—was looking out over a finished
field. Hay bunches stretched from one end to the other. It was a
sight to behold and an accomplishment to be rightly proud of. At
day's end, the four of us stood at the end of the field leaning on
our forks. Pa didn't say much, perhaps a comment or two about
how good or poor the crop was compared to last year. Mostly, I
believe, as I think back now, he wanted us to appreciate the joy
of a job well done and to see the results stretched before us in
long, straight rows.

If the weather held, by the next afternoon we were pitching
the hay bunches onto our steel-wheeled wagon and hauling the
load to the barn. Then we pitched off the hay, one forkful at a
time. Two of us worked on the wagon, pitching the hay through
the barn door; two of us worked in the barn, pitching the hay
into the corners.

This job changed when we got the larger barn, with its mechanical
hayfork that deposited the hay into the haymows with far less
human effort. But Swendryznski's hay baler changed haymaking
much more than the mechanical hayfork. When you used a baler,
the hay had to be raked with a side-delivery rake that made long
ropes of hay that wound around the field—different from the
dump rake where the hay stretched across the field. After raking,
the hay dried for a few hours and then the hay baler picked up
the long ropes and formed them into bales. No longer did we
use pitchforks and muscle to bunch the hay; the baler did the
hard work. After we tied hay wire around a new bale, the baler
deposited it back on the ground. Later, we drove around the field
picking up the bales, many of which weighed over a hundred

pounds. We hauled them to the barn, stacked them on the elevator, and watched it mechanically lift the load into the haymows, where several men neatly stacked the bales. Less dust, less work, less time involved.

But was baled hay as good as loose hay? Would cattle eat it? Was the cost of having it baled—ten cents a bale, paid to John Swendryznski—worth it? The immediate answer was yes, cows fed eagerly on baled hay, and it seemed well worth the extra cost. But in those early years of hay balers, with farmers storing much more weight in the same area, some barns collapsed. And some cattle began exhibiting mysterious health problems. As it turned out, many had ingested pieces of hay wire. In a few years, machinery manufacturers began producing hay balers that tied baler with twine. And farmers learned to reinforce their barns to prevent them from collapsing under the extra weight.

The transition was made. Loose hay and all the steps involved in making it had become a part of farming history. Within a few years, all the neighbors, except one, baled their hay. The same farmer who refused to plant alfalfa also said loose hay was better for your cows, and as far as I know, he never changed.

CHAPTER 18

⌇

Ma's Projects

Strawberries—$.20 per quart
(sold to Wild Rose Mercantile)
Strawberries—$.10 per quart (pick your own)
Baby chicks—$45.00
Coal for brooder stove—$4.40
Chick feed—$2.40
Chicken wire—$2.90
Garden seeds—$2.25

My ma was usually easy to get along with. But at strawberry-picking time, she became a field general—likely because she was all German and had in her inheritance the ability to organize and supervise and keep everybody on the straight and narrow.

The strawberry patch, west of the barn in a field between the white pine windbreak and the oak woods, covered about one acre. Depending on an early or late spring, Ma's strawberries started to ripen mid-June, sometimes earlier, sometimes a few days later. Around the first of June, we looked for the first ripe strawberry of the season. Ma decided when enough were ripe, and she phoned folks who had picked berries other years.

Ma worked out a flag system for marking the rows, and she assigned one to each picker. "Here's your row," Ma would say when the picker arrived. Some pickers—new ones, usually—might stray from their assigned row to one that appeared to have more and bigger strawberries. Ma's field-general eye watched for such behavior.

Like a hawk swooping down on unsuspecting prey, she confronted the errant strawberry picker and got her back on her assigned row. The delinquents were mostly women. Men knew better than to disobey Ma. Men stayed where Ma put them, even when the berries in their row were scrawny and in short supply.

Strawberry picking usually went on well past the Fourth of July, and Ma insisted on supervising the strawberry patch full time, keeping pickers on their rows—and chastising them if they heaped up their boxes too full. Ma sold the berries by the boxful (a quart), and she hated it when a picker heaped the box, in her opinion, with too many berries. Ma spent so much time in the strawberry patch that Aunt Louise, who lived in Wild Rose, would come out to the farm to cook our meals and answer the phone.

While Ma supervised, Pa, my brothers, and I—when we weren't making hay or hoeing—picked strawberries for our table and for sale. The Wild Rose Mercantile bought as many picked berries as we could provide; Pa took a crate (sixteen quarts) to the Merc a couple times a week.

We also ate our share of fresh strawberries. We added them to our cereal in the morning. We made strawberry sandwiches at noon (mash fresh strawberries and sprinkle with sugar, then take a thick slice of homemade bread, spread about one-eighth inch of butter across it, cover it with the strawberries, then put another hunk of buttered bread on top). We ate strawberries for supper served on shortcake, the berries piled high. And once or twice a week, Ma baked a strawberry pie. She even talked once about making strawberry wine, but that seemed a waste when we had so many better ways of consuming this wonderful fruit. Before electricity arrived on our farm, Ma canned strawberry sauce in quart jars; after electricity, she froze them in our freezer.

Just as fast as the strawberry season started, it ended. In mid-
July, we picked a few little, sweet berries for another week or so,
but the big, juicy ones were gone. Ma, the field general of the
strawberry patch, went back in the kitchen, and we went on to
the next summer project.

Along with the strawberry patch, Ma was in charge of the chickens.
We all helped with feeding, gathering the eggs, and the like, but
the chickens were Ma's project in every respect. She decided what
kind we would raise—White Leghorns for eggs, White Rocks for
meat—and she supervised the daily gathering and cleaning of
the eggs; she sold them, traded them, and recorded the money
earned; and she alone spent the egg money—on clothes, school
supplies, and Christmas presents. Ma was as proud of her chickens and the money earned from eggs as Pa was proud of his cows
and money earned from milk.

Ma ordered the chicks from a hatchery in the southern part
of the state. Before the chicks arrived, Pa and Ma readied the
brooder house, a small building near the barn. The brooder equipment included a little coal-burning stove with a metal hood some
six feet across. The baby chicks would huddle under the hood to
keep warm. The brooder was also equipped with a feeder full of
chick feed and a glass jar that served as a waterer.

When Ma's order came in, George Collum, the depot agent in
Wild Rose, would call on the telephone. "Your chicks are here,"
he'd say. Ma smiled when she hung up.

One year, I rode with Pa to the depot to pick up the chicks.
It was a blustery day in early April, with snowflakes flying on a
cold, northwest wind. The depot, located on the west side of Wild
Rose near the railroad tracks, had three rooms: a tiny office with
telegraph equipment and a window for selling tickets; a large
waiting room heated with a big coal-burning stove; and an even
larger, unheated freight room where the depot agent temporarily

stored incoming and outgoing freight. But Mr. Collum would never store a shipment of chicks in the cold freight room.

As Pa pulled open the front door and we entered the waiting room, the sound of peeping baby chicks engulfed us. The sound came from cardboard boxes stacked near the stove, each little chick letting us know of its presence.

"Hello, Herman," Mr. Collum said as he came out of his office. "Let's see, I've got the paperwork for your chicks right here." He sorted through a sheaf of papers he carried. "This bunch of chicks came in on the morning train. Looks like everyone around here will be raising chickens this year. Yours are the White Leghorns, that box over there."

"Sure are noisy," I said.

"Expect they're hungry," Mr. Collum said. "Been on the train since early this morning."

Pa carried the heavy cardboard box to the Plymouth and set it on the back seat. It had "baby chicks" written on it in large print and held one hundred of them, each scarcely larger than the egg from which they came.

When we arrived home, Pa carried the box into the kitchen and put it on the floor by the stove. Ma wanted to make sure the chicks were warm and healthy before taking them out to the brooder house. The kitchen filled with the sound of a hundred baby chicks.

Ma removed the box's cover and we all looked at the little balls of yellow fluff, each with its beak open, peeping as loudly as it could. "Aren't they just the cutest little things," Ma said. My brothers and I wanted to take some out and play with them, but Ma said they'd had enough excitement for one day.

Later that afternoon, when the brooder stove had been started and the feeders and waterers filled, Pa carried the box to the brooder house and gently set the chicks free to wander the building. Soon, they gathered under the warmth of the brooder-stove hood. Later, they lined up at the little feeders and stuck their beaks in the purple water; Ma had put a pill in the water to ward off any disease.

By fall, the chicks became chickens and moved to the main chicken house, which was a low, long building with a wall of south-facing windows located just west of our farmhouse. Ma's chickens provided a goodly share of the chores my brothers and I did every day. About one hundred twenty-five to one hundred fifty layers in the main chicken house produced up to eight dozen eggs a day, and us boys gathered these eggs every evening. Ma counted and sold eggs by the dozen. An egg man came around once a week and bought Ma's eggs, which she had packed in twelve dozen crates. She saved enough eggs for trading at the Wild Rose Mercantile on Saturday night, and she always kept a few dozen on hand for town relatives and friends.

Ma kept a careful record of every dozen eggs sold and every nickel of egg money spent. She also recorded the money earned from selling old chickens; those that no longer laid eggs were butchered and sold. Besides the monetary reward, Ma's chickens provided a never-ending supply of fresh eggs and a cellar shelf of canned chicken. But my favorite part of raising chickens was the sound of peeping baby chicks every year, signaling the arrival of spring.

Another of Ma's projects, the garden, provided us with a constant supply of fresh vegetables, from the first radishes of spring to winter squash and pumpkins. Ma also busied herself all summer canning peas, carrots, green beans, and sweet corn. And when the cabbage came in, we helped her make a big crock of sauerkraut that lasted most of the winter.

Ma's garden taught me and my brothers to appreciate the wonderful taste of fresh vegetables, prepared but a few minutes from harvesting. We also loved canned vegetables on cold, snowy winter days, when Ma's garden lay buried deep in snow and she longingly waited for her seed catalogs to arrive in the mailbox. Ma looked for the catalogs in February, when the snow piled up high against the house and morning temperatures stayed below zero for days on end. I remember she especially anticipated the Old's catalog from Madison, and Jung's catalog from Randolph.

"Gotta be careful where you order garden seeds," Ma said. "You get hold of one of them southern seed growers and your garden won't amount to much. Need to have the seeds from the North."

When the catalogs arrived, she'd read them at night after chores, sitting at the kitchen table with her back to the woodstove, studying each page by the light of a kerosene lamp. Sometimes, she acted as if this was the first time she'd ever looked at a seed catalog. While my brothers and I did our homework, Ma decided what garden varieties to order. Sometimes she'd ask Pa what he thought, but not often. Ma was in charge of the garden, and she ordered what she wanted.

Seed catalogs can be deceiving. Seldom do you grow a crop as nice as what is pictured in the catalog, no matter if it's cucumbers or green beans, tomatoes or sweet corn. I suspect Ma knew this as well as anyone, but she was a good gardener and I imagine she looked on those pictures as a kind of challenge. *If somebody else can grow tomatoes that look this good,* she likely thought, *then I probably can, too.* And she often did.

Ma worked on the seed order for a couple nights, wrote a check, mailed the envelope, and waited like a kid for the order to arrive. She didn't let on what she was doing, but we knew she had an eye on each day's mail delivery, looking for a little package of garden seeds. When the order arrived, Ma examined each packet, no doubt imagining what these tiny pieces of wonder would produce this season.

Ma stored the seed packets in some special place I never knew about, except the tomato seeds. These she kept on the dining room clock shelf, alongside special letters and egg money, to plant on St. Patrick's Day. No matter what day March 17 fell on, even Sunday, Ma took the tomato seeds down from the clock shelf and planted them in flower pots.

"Everything about St. Patrick's Day is green," she said. "Proper day to plant tomato seeds so the plants are big enough to set out in the garden when the weather warms up." Just like she waited for the catalogs and then her seed order, Ma kept a careful eye on the newly planted tomato seeds, watching for the first green to appear above the brown soil. Those first fragile tomato shoots marked the official beginning of another gardening season.

Not many days after the snow disappeared and the sun warmed the ground, pie plant began shoving out of the ground. Pie plant is an old-fashioned name for rhubarb, and it was one of the few plants in Ma's garden that she didn't plant from seed each year.

A few clusters of pie plant grew near the pump house, on the southeast corner where the ground warmed up soonest in spring. One thing about pie plant, once you see it poking out of the ground, you better keep an eye on it. Before you know it, when you're all tangled up with spring cleaning and such, the stalks have gotten too big, tough, bitter, and not fit for eating.

I don't recall that Ma ever let that happen. She wasn't one to allow anything to go to waste. She was out there pulling pie plant stems when they were just right. She claimed we kids didn't know how to judge a pie plant. "Takes an experienced eye to know when to pull pie plant," she said. Tell you the truth, we didn't mind. It meant one less job we had to do. The growing season of field crops provided plenty of work.

First thing Ma made from pie plant was sauce. I can't say, as a kid, I cared much for it. Too sour. But even Pa insisted that we eat it. Something about it being a spring tonic, a cleanser of the system.

Along the way, often as a surprise, Ma would bake a rhubarb pie. Rhubarb pie tastes as different from rhubarb sauce as newly rendered lard from ice cream. A close relative to pie was rhubarb crisp—mighty tasty, too, but not up to the qualities of pie. Ma's rhubarb pie was delicious, right up there with apple and cherry and even lemon meringue. I never questioned why old-timers referred to rhubarb as pie plant; Ma's rhubarb pie made it clear.

Unlike pie plant, Ma didn't like cooking with summer squash, which we had in abundance one summer. She couldn't wrap her mind around a squash that wouldn't keep for at least half the winter, like our regular winter squash. Aunt Louise suggested Ma fry some of the summer squash, like you'd fry potatoes. Ma couldn't see much sense to the idea—"Who'd want to fry squash?" was her reply to Aunt Louise. But Ma tried Aunt Louise's recipe, and one day she served some shriveled-up, deeply browned mystery slices on our plates.

"Summer squash," Ma said. "You'll like it. Aunt Louise said you'd like it." But Ma's voice had no conviction. You could tell she didn't think much of her new fried-squash recipe, and four others sitting around the table agreed. Fried squash couldn't hold a candle to fried red potatoes, fried onions, or just about anything else fried. Those browned, shriveled slices tasted like fried shoe-leather; in fact, I think Pa would have preferred shoe-leather.

Later, Aunt Arvilla suggested shredding the summer squash and using it in cake, breads, or muffins. "Makes really good bread," Aunt Arvilla said. "Nice and moist. Doesn't taste anything like squash either." Ma promised to try one of Aunt Arvilla's recipes, but I don't recall that she ever did.

For all the fresh vegetables and delicious pies, Ma's garden produced plenty of unwanted products, from summer squash to additional farm work for us boys. Shucking peas was one of those jobs. Ma usually announced at the noon dinner table when the peas were ready and that she needed help shucking. Ma picked most of the peas herself, to make sure the peapods filled out just right and the immature ones remained on the vine.

She'd appear with a big wash pan heaping full of plump pods, and set it under the elm tree in front of the house. I don't remember how we decided which of us boys helped shuck and which continued hoeing; maybe we took turns. To shuck peas, we sat with the huge pile of peas on a little table in front of us and a smaller pan on each of our laps. Ma taught me how to squeeze a peapod open so the fat, green peas popped out and dropped into the pan. After I'd done about the fiftieth peapod, the novelty of the task wore thin. By that time, I'd gotten past any remedial lessons Ma figured I needed on how to do the job properly. I just continued popping one boring pod after the other.

Of course, shucking peas was far from the farm's worst job, especially when the alternative was hoeing potatoes in the hot sun. And as boring as shucking peas could be, it had some pluses. As the oldest kid in the family, I didn't have much time to talk with Ma. I was always with Pa, either doing barn chores or fieldwork. Shucking peas gave me a chance to be with her.

One year, about the time I began feeling sorry for myself sitting there popping peas, Ma asked me a question that took my mind completely off peapods.

"Ever thought what you want to do when you finish school?"

"Nope," I replied. "Can't say I have." I would be entering high school in Wild Rose in the fall, with only four more years of schooling. Ma hadn't stopped shucking when she asked, so I kept piling peas in my pan when I answered.

We talked about what I wanted to do—about finishing high school and then taking up farming full time, about buying some calves that would be the start of my own dairy herd. The possibility of going to college after high school never came up. There were long pauses in between when we just sat shucking in silence. We talked about when she was a little girl and shucked peas with her mother. We talked about the weather. We talked about my grandparents—Ma's parents, who had both died when I was seven. She said how much she still thought of them and missed them. She told me about the German Lutheran parochial school she had attended in Kellner, Wisconsin, where the teachers didn't allow anyone to speak or write in English.

Before I knew it, the pan of peapods sat empty and each of our basins was heaped with fresh peas—wonderful-tasting, sweet green peas that we would eat every day until the plants produced no more pods. I had learned a lot about Ma I didn't know before—about her early schooling, about her growing-up years on a farm, and about her parents, my grandparents. I suspect she learned some new things about me, too—how I looked forward to finishing high school and taking up farming, how much I wanted some milk cows I could call my own. And it all happened because of a pan of fresh garden peas.

CHAPTER 19

᠍᠍᠍᠍᠍᠍᠍᠍᠍᠍᠍᠍᠍

Ma's Illness

Hospital and doctor bills—$311.75

My family depended on Ma more than we knew. She kept the
house in order, cooked our meals, washed and ironed our clothes,
cared for the chickens, and maintained a huge vegetable garden.
She kept track of all the farm's expenses and income in her record books. She baked, canned, and traded eggs for groceries
during our regular Saturday night trips to town. She cooked for
the threshing and silo-filling crews, and provided meals for relatives who dropped in at mealtimes expecting something to eat.
Ma made sure us boys finished our chores on time. She nursed
us when we were sick, helped us with our homework, and always
listened when we had a problem or concern. She did all this with
a quiet, no-nonsense efficiency. She almost never raised her voice,
but when she did, you knew you had stepped over the line.

I never thought much about any of this until the day Pa took
Ma to Dr. Hadden in Wild Rose. Ma had been complaining about
trouble swallowing, and Pa finally had convinced her to see the
doctor. When they returned home, they said little. I could see the
news was not good; it was written all over their faces.

That evening, around the supper table, Pa broke the news to us.

"Ma's got to have her goiter out," he said. "So she can swallow better."

Ma sat quietly, looking down at her hands. My brothers and I all knew about goiters because our teacher made us take "goiter pills" at school. They were chocolate-flavored iodine pills. If you didn't get enough iodine, your thyroid gland in your neck would swell up into a goiter.

"They'll do the operation at St. Agnes Hospital in Fond du Lac," Pa said. Fond du Lac lay only about seventy-five miles east of our farm, at the southern end of Lake Winnebago, but in those days it might as well have been five hundred miles. I had never been there, and Ma and Pa had been only a couple times.

"They've scheduled the operation for next week," Pa said.

"What will we do without Ma?" Duck asked. He had a long look on his face.

"We'll make do," Pa said. "We'll make do. But you'll have more chores than usual."

"How . . . how long will she be gone?" Murf asked hesitantly.

"If the operation goes well, about two weeks."

Ma still looked at her hands, but I could see tears in her eyes.

The following Monday morning, we drove Ma to the Wild Rose train depot, where she met her sister Louise. Ma tried to keep a positive attitude, but she was having a tough time. She was usually talkative, but this morning she said little, except to remind us of our chores, how she wished she didn't have to go away, and that we should help out Pa. She gave each of us a hug and told us to be sure and help Pa with the work. Then she and Aunt Louise climbed on the train. The steam locomotive whistled twice and belched an immense cloud of black smoke from its stack. The huge driver wheels began turning. Ma waved out the window, and we waved back—my brothers and I standing in front, Pa standing behind us, his crumpled cap in his hands. He had the most sorrowful look on his face I had ever seen.

"Let's go, boys," Pa said, as the train disappeared around the corner.

We drove back to the farm in silence, each of us with our own thoughts of what we would do with Ma away. After all, she had never been away from the family overnight.

"I've arranged for a girl from the other side of town to stay with us and help with the cooking and washing," Pa said. "Boots is her name, Boots Karsney. She's coming on Wednesday."

Pa fixed dinner for us that noon. None of us had an appetite, which was good because Pa was an awful cook. We ate burned fried potatoes, scorched fried bologna, and thankfully some bread Ma had baked the day before.

The next day several neighbors brought over casseroles, cakes, and pies, and we knew we'd survive until Boots arrived. She came on Wednesday, dropped off by her father, I guessed. She carried a sack of her things and wore a concerned look on her face. Boots was sixteen years old, not much taller than five feet, with closely bobbed black hair and a pleasant smile. She probably hadn't spent a night away from home, and here she was several miles from home and expected to do the cooking and washing for Pa, my brothers, and me.

Boots couldn't cook as well as Ma, but her meals were so many times better than Pa's that none of us murmured the least bit of criticism. Soon we established a new routine, different from when Ma was home. Boots did her best, but nobody could take the place of Ma. Boots didn't know—how could she?—that Duck wouldn't eat vegetables without encouragement. Ma always sorted our clothes after washing and ironing them; Boots piled the clothes on the table and we sorted through them, looking for our own. When we tussled with each other, Ma was not there to establish order and mete out punishment. Boots seemed baffled when we wrestled, not knowing what to do. To her credit, she never tattled on us to Pa.

We all missed Ma, from the moment we got up in the morning until we crawled into our beds at night. My brothers and I wondered how Ma was doing; Pa told us nothing about how the operation had gone. Finally, Pa told us on Friday that we were driving to Fond du Lac the next day to see Ma in the hospital and that we'd leave right after morning chores.

The trip took us all morning. Our Plymouth had a top speed of fifty miles per hour, and as Pa said, top speed meant driving downhill with the wind at our back. The car's rebuilt engine didn't work right; in fact, if you turned it off, it wouldn't start again for a half hour or more until it had cooled off. So any trip was an adventure.

Finally we arrived in Fond du Lac, and after asking directions at a gas station (making sure to keep the car running), we found the immense brick building that housed St. Agnes Hospital. Inside the hospital, I was struck by the size of the place and how everything was white—the walls, the ceilings, the reception desk, the clothes the nurses wore (I assumed they were nurses). The quiet reminded me of church, except people were scurrying around and talking in quiet voices. We walked up to the desk and the Sister asked how she could help. Pa said that we were here to see Mrs. Apps. The Sister looked through some papers and gave us the name of the room.

"But no children are allowed to visit patients," she said. Darrel's lower lip started to quiver.

"I want the boys to see their ma," Pa said with a firm voice. He put both of his huge hands on the desk and looked the Sister in the eye.

"I think we can make an exception this once," the Sister said, smiling at me and my brothers.

We walked down the long hospital hall, looking for Ma's room number and smelling what we had never smelled before. It was a sweetish, medicinal smell—sort of like the smell of a newly opened tin of Watkin's salve. Finding the room, Pa gently knocked on the door and we entered. He walked in first, then me, then Darrel, and then Donald. Pa had told us beforehand that we must take off our caps, so there we stood, the four of us, with caps in hand.

Ma sat propped up in a big bed, her face as white as the bed clothing. A huge bandage stretched from one side of her neck to the other. She smiled, and Pa asked how she was doing.

I could barely make out Ma's response. In a whisper, she said she thought she was getting better and was looking forward to coming home.

We all said we wanted her home, too. Duck blurted out that Pa was an awful cook and that Boots was better, but not near as good as her. Ma smiled; apparently Pa's awful cooking skills weren't news to her. We told her about the chickens and how good they were doing, about the garden and how well it was growing, and that we were doing our chores without being reminded. She smiled and whispered how much she had been counting on the three of us to help out Pa.

We hadn't been in Ma's room more than fifteen minutes when a Sister came in and said it was time for us to leave. We each walked by Ma and said goodbye, and then we were back in the Plymouth on our way to the farm.

"Is Ma gonna die?" Darrel asked. His bottom lip was quivering again.

"I don't know," Pa said. And that's all he said as we drove on, no one speaking until we got to the town of Neshkoro, twenty miles from home. We stopped for gas and waited a half hour at the gas station for the engine to cool. Pa went into a grocery store and bought a box of saltine crackers—we called them "salty crackers"—and a ring of bologna.

"This will be our supper," Pa said. "I gave Boots the weekend off." He sliced up the bologna and passed around the crackers.

Back in the car, we continued on home. A sadder foursome you have never seen.

At home, my brothers and I grew to love and depend on Boots, and our appreciation for her strengthened our appreciation for Ma. We came to see how much we took for granted. And we knew Boots cared about us boys and Pa, too.

One night at the supper table, Pa said we boys should take Boots swimming in Chain O' Lake. The next afternoon was warm and sunny. When we finished washing and drying the noon dishes—we all helped, even Pa—we walked the mile and a half to the lake. We had a grand time, the four of us, splashing, trying to swim, fighting with long stringy weeds, and looking for leeches that latched onto a toe and stayed there until we yanked them off. We discovered that Boots was still just a kid on this day when she didn't have to act like a grown-up.

A week later, Pa told us Ma was coming home. We were all so happy to see her, even though several more weeks passed before she regained enough strength so we could say goodbye to Boots.

Ma's illness brought home in a powerful way how farm families depended on each other, especially on the mothers whose work was often taken for granted. That spring and summer, my brothers and I—and I suspect Pa, too—gained a powerful new appreciation and love for Ma.

CHAPTER 20

↬

Pickle Patch

No. 1 cucumbers—$15.00 per hundredweight
No. 2 cucumbers—$7.50 per hundredweight
No. 3 cucumbers—$3.00 per hundredweight
No. 4 cucumbers—$.50 per hundredweight

My brothers and I hated and loved the pickle patch at the same time. It was a mean job, hoeing around those fragile little vines under the hot sun, and once the plants began bearing fruit, picking took six weeks of backbreaking, finger-staining, sweat-dripping work. But Pa let us keep the money earned from our pickings, and some days we earned up to fifteen dollars apiece. Compared to working for a neighbor at a dollar a day—the common farmhand wage—working in the pickle patch was like mining gold.

Pa planted a pickle patch every year, sometimes as much as two acres but generally around an acre. When we planted a crop in a small field, say three acres or less, Pa called it a patch.

One time, a Wisconsin Rapids relative told Pa he was wrong to call our pickle patch a pickle patch. "What in blazes is wrong in calling that patch of pickles what it is?" Pa asked in exasperation. He often lost his patience with city relatives who knew not a wit about farming, gardening, or anything else that took place outside their houses or the paper mills where they worked.

"You should call it a cucumber patch. Cucumbers become pickles once they've been processed," the relative said in his high-minded way. "Like dill pickles and sweet and sour pickles."

"Well, out here in the country, this patch of ground is a pickle patch," Pa said, looking the city relative square in the eye. And that was the end of the conversation. Pa was not much for city folks telling him anything, especially what to call his pickle patch.

Pa switched the pickle patch to a different field about every year. "Keeps the disease problems down," he said. He was right, of course. Every spring, my brothers and I waited to see what piece of ground Pa selected. We preferred one near some oak trees so we could cool off in the shade when we were supposed to be picking cucumbers. Too often, Pa selected a patch of ground tucked up against a pine windbreak, and during the hot days of summer, not a whisper of a breeze trickled through the thick white pines. In these stifling conditions, my brothers and I hoed the pickle patch until the vines grew large enough to shade out most of the weeds. The cucumbers wouldn't amount to anything unless we chopped the ragweed, pigweed, thistles, and quack grass that grew anywhere and crowded out anything.

In late July, the cucumbers began bearing, and picking season began. Cucumbers are not pleasant to pick. They have sharp little spines; they stain your fingers and create crusty brown layers on your hands that not even the strongest Lava soap will take off. A few of my friends wore rubber gloves to pick cucumbers, but nobody in my family did. Pa considered it sissy, and besides, it was difficult to pick the littlest cukes wearing gloves.

We picked every other day during pickle season, which ran to the end of August. At day's end, we delivered the cucumbers to the H. J. Heinz salting station. It was located in Wild Rose, back of the sawmill. The highlight of a day's picking was hauling the half dozen or more full gunny sacks to the station, where we lifted the bags up on the receiving floor and watched one of the Heinz guys dump them into the sorter. The cucumbers tumbled into wooden bushel boxes according to their size. The little cukes were number ones, the biggest, number fours.

The station paid according to size. The smallest cucumbers, about an inch long, fetched the highest price per pound. Problem was it took a bunch of those little cukes to weigh a pound. The largest ones, six inches or longer, fetched only five cents a pound. It took only a few of the big ones to make a pound. We took every cucumber that wasn't yellow—a sign it was too ripe—to the station.

On a good day, if you hustled and didn't spend too much time drinking water in the shade, you could earn up to fifteen dollars. Other days, you might only earn five dollars, depending on the rainfall and temperature. We spent most of our earnings on school clothes, but what was left could go for a bike or some books— those things my brothers and I always wanted but the family generally couldn't afford. We might also buy a rifle or a hunting knife; hunting season was in the fall and early winter, when the summer work was done and we had a little spare time after school and on weekends. Pa also insisted we save some of the money.

By late August, the vines looked bedraggled from all the handling. Cooler nights slowed production as well. Now we picked every three days, or even every four days, and toted only a bag or two to the salting station.

The season ended just about the time school started in the fall. With our cucumber money, my brothers and I could afford new bib overalls, new shirts, and shiny new pencil boxes for our first day of school. We felt sorry for those kids who didn't have pickle patches, but not too sorry, as we remembered the hot days of summer when those same kids swam or played ball while we toiled in the pickle patch.

Occasionally, we complained to Pa about our situation compared to those kids who didn't have pickle patches.

"Those kids aren't learning how to work," Pa was quick to answer. "Everybody should learn how to work."

He may have had a point.

CHAPTER 21

⟿

Threshing

Farmall H tractor—$1,750.00
Used threshing machine (one-half interest)—$141.25
Drive belt—$49.00
Combining—$6.50

The first major purchase Pa made when the war ended was a new tractor, a Farmall H that had been on steel wheels and converted to rubber tires. During the war, new farm equipment was next to impossible to buy, especially tractors. Now tractors became available, and we had a new red one in our yard.

But Pa and the neighbors still depended on Milton Vromen, a farmer from outside the area, to come in during threshing season and make the rounds with his threshing machine. Vromen threshed five hundred to one thousand bushels of oats at each farm. Depending on the size of the harvest and the weather, one job took anywhere from a day to nearly three days, and the farmer paid Vromen anywhere from twenty-five to fifty dollars for his services.

Two years in a row, Vromen was a couple weeks late to our neighborhood. He was so busy threshing fields on the prairie to our west that he didn't show up on time. Grain bundles standing in a shock—be it oats, rye, or wheat—can take only so much rain before the grain begins to spoil. In the worst situations, the grain seeds begin to grow while the straw turns musty and starts to rot. Both years, Pa lost a goodly amount of his grain harvest to spoilage.

One spring day, Pa got to talking at the gristmill with Bill Miller, our nearest neighbor to the south. Bill had lost part of his grain crop the previous year, too.

"We outta buy our own threshing machine," Pa said.

"Yeah," Bill agreed. "We outta."

"Can't be a big one, though," Pa said. All they had to power the machine was Pa's Farmall H and Bill's John Deere B.

"Probably a 22-incher," Bill said. "I know my B will run such a machine just fine."

"I'm not so sure about that," Pa said. "You only got two cylinders in that green machine."

"Only need two," Bill said. "You just wait, you'll see that my B runs a threshing machine better by far than your H."

Mind you, all this talk about whose tractor was better and they hadn't even bought a threshing machine yet. Of course, all the farmers in our neighborhood constantly argued about who owned the best tractor and had done so since the first one was unloaded from the dealer's truck.

Our own Farmall H, which Pa had paid for with $1,750 cash, could do so much more than our old converted Ford truck-tractor. Two big improvements were a belt pulley and a two-row cultivator. Our new Farmall could power a portable feed mill or a circle saw for cutting wood. And it could cultivate corn and potatoes two rows at a time. Although Pa soon sold our homemade tractor, painted silver so it was quite distinctive, he kept our team of draft horses until they died several years later.

Pa scanned the farm papers, especially the *Wisconsin Agriculturist*, until he spotted a used McCormick 22-inch threshing machine for sale. The size referred to the width of the cylinder, the main threshing element in the machine. A threshing machine could be 22-inch, 28-inch, even 32-inch. A larger machine would handle more grain in a shorter time but required a bigger tractor than either Bill Miller or Pa had.

A fellow south of Wautoma had the threshing machine for sale. He wanted three hundred dollars, a sizable chunk of money in 1946. After some considerable haggling, during which Pa pointed out that the main drive belt was missing, they agreed on $282.50, with Pa paying half and Bill the other half. The purchase price included delivery, which took the better part of a day. Pulled by the seller's old Fordson tractor, the steel-wheeled threshing machine lumbered along at under five miles per hour.

It was a sight to behold when that monster of a machine pulled into our dooryard. The fellow yanked the draw pin and dropped the drawbar to the ground.

"There she is," the fellow said. "You'll like her. She's a sweet machine."

Bill came over that night after chores, and he and Pa and my brothers and I crawled all over the thresher and inside it, too. We cranked the handle that worked the straw blower, and we put the grain chute into place and tried out the bagger. We unfolded the grain bundle feeder in front, where the bundles are tossed on their way into the great machine's maw. We sorted out the pile of belts of various sizes and lengths, trying to figure out which belt went over which pulley and whether it went clockwise or counterclockwise, requiring a twist in the belt.

The next day, Pa drove to the Sears store in Berlin, where he bought a new drive belt. Pa and Bill agreed that Pa would own the drive belt, because he figured one day he might buy some other equipment that required a belt, such as a hammer mill for grinding cow feed. Threshing season was still a couple weeks away, but Pa and Bill told all our neighbors about their threshing machine and offered to make the rounds. They planned to use the H to run the machine every other day, and the B on alternate days. Everyone seemed pleased to hear they wouldn't have to wait for Milton Vromen's big rig to come down into the hills from the prairie.

For several evenings, Pa and Bill greased, tightened, and even replaced the bearings in a couple of pulley housings. A better-than average mechanic, Bill made sure the machine was in tip-top shape.

One night, Bill came over with his John Deere B to see how well it would power the machine. This was the moment Pa had been waiting for. The competition among tractor owners was fierce, especially between John Deere and Farmall advocates. Pa had already secretly backed his H into the drive belt a couple days earlier, and everything seemed to work well—at least when it wasn't threshing. Once the men tossed oat bundles into the machine and the actual threshing began, everything might be different.

Bill backed his B into position. Pa slipped the drive belt over the threshing machine's main pulley and over the tractor's drive pulley. Bill backed slowly, tightening the belt. The John Deere idled, *pop, pop*. It was crucial that the threshing machine's main pulley and the tractor's drive pulley lined up perfectly and the belt had just the right amount of tension; otherwise the belt might run off the tractor pulley, creating considerable havoc and possibly hurting someone.

Bill backed up perfectly, and everything was properly aligned.

"Let her go," Pa said. Bill engaged the pulley and slowly pushed on the hand clutch while giving the B more gas. The pulley starting turning, and the giant threshing machine awakened as its many belts and pulleys began turning.

Pop, pop, pop, the John Deere reported with authority as the threshing machine got up to speed.

"Works just fine," Bill said proudly. "Ain't much these John Deeres can't do."

Pa didn't say anything. He knew the true test would come on the first day of threshing when the men fed oat bundles into the machine.

Threshing season began a couple weeks later, appropriately at Bill's farm. When the threshing crew arrived, Bill already had his John Deere backed into the belt and ready to start.

Soon, George Kolka and his team of buckskin horses pulled the first bundle wagon up to the threshing machine. Bill got the thresher up to speed. George, one of the best bundle pitchers in our neighborhood, started tossing oat bundles—head first, one after the other—onto the feeder.

Bundle pitchers like George set the bar for young guys like myself. Threshing day was an opportunity to show your stuff, to demonstrate that you could work as hard and as long as anyone else on the threshing crew. You demonstrated your manliness best by pitching bundles from a bundle wagon into the maw of the threshing machine, one bundle after the other, never faltering, never losing the rhythm that was necessary to keep the threshing machine running evenly. The way you knew you were doing a good job was to hear nothing, no comments, no "good job"— nothing like that. You knew you had been accepted as a man when your dad didn't criticize you or a friend didn't poke fun at you. You were praised with silence. The respect you saw in the faces of the men you worked with, who now knew they could depend on you to do a man's job. It was a wonderful feeling.

George continued to toss bundles into the feeder. So far, so good. The John Deere popped louder as its governor opened, but the thresher was doing its job. Oat straw flew out the blower pipe, and newly threshed oats accumulated in the little grain box above the bagger chute.

But a few bundles must have had some morning dew, because the thresher began to growl, as a threshing machine tends to do when it tries to thresh damp grain. The more the machine growled, the louder the John Deere popped and the more the drive belt slapped. Bill gave the B more throttle, but it didn't help. The belt was about to jump off the pulleys.

"Stop pitching, George!" Bill yelled. He shut down the machine, which was now plugged with threshed and partially threshed grain from one end to the other.

No words were spoken as Bill drove his John Deere B under a tree and Pa backed his Farmall H into place. The crew spent a half hour or so unplugging the machine, then continued threshing. The four-cylinder H purred along with no belt-slapping or decrease in speed.

The men didn't say much to Bill about the incident, aside from a couple backhanded questions at the dinner table—"Hear the B couldn't take it?" But soon enough everyone in the neighborhood knew about it, whether they had been on the threshing crew or not. And whenever a group of farmers started debating which was better, a Farmall or a John Deere, someone always referred to the day the H handled the threshing machine and the B failed.

A few years later, Vilas Olson, a neighbor south of us, purchased an Allis-Chalmers grain combine. It was orange, like all Allis-Chalmers equipment, and in one sweep around an oat field, it cut, threshed, and cleaned the grain, tossing the straw out behind. Its name came from combining a grain binder—which cut grain and bound it in bundles—with a threshing machine that separated the grain kernels from the straw.

No longer did Vilas Olson participate in the threshing ring that traveled from farm to farm every August. Olson harvested his own oats with his new combine. Neighbors found little good to say about Olson's new machine. But most, at one time or another, found an excuse to stop by his farm and see the machine work. They stood by watching it move around the field, slicing off ripe oat plants.

They didn't say much to Olson about his machine, but to each other they couldn't stop talking:

"Another newfangled machine. Never catch on here."

"Land's too hilly around here, too stony for such a fancy contraption."

"How's the thing gonna thresh grain on a side hill? Tell me that."

"First big stone he hits, and that'll be the end. Smash that thing all to hell."

"Look at all the straw he's wasting. Has the sickle bar set so high to miss the stones, he cuts only half the stalk."

"Takes a lot of power to pull that thing. Makes his big Massey Harris tractor really talk."

"Oats on top of the hills ripen before those in the hollow. If he waits for the hollow oats to ripen, the overripe oats on the hilltops will be falling off."

Olson had hoped to do some custom grain harvesting, but for the first couple of years, not one farmer hired him to cut their oats. Not one. To a person, they were convinced that that the superior way to harvest grain was to cut it with a binder, shock it by hand to let it dry, and then thresh it with a threshing machine.

One year, Pa hired Olson to combine his clover seed. Pa had planted five acres of red clover and let it go to seed. Pa regularly planted clover for hay, but not for seed. An ordinary threshing machine can't hull clover, because it can't be adjusted to thresh seeds as small as clover—smaller than a radish seed. The old way of harvesting was to cut the clover, pile it in bunches to dry, and haul it to some farmer who owned a clover huller, which looks like a threshing machine but smaller. On the other hand, Olson's combine could be adjusted to hull clover and do the entire job, just like he harvested oats.

Together, Olson and Pa decided when the clover had ripened and dried enough to harvest. On a hot, dry summer day, Olson pulled into our yard with his combine. Pa hoped none of the neighbors would see the combine, because it would thoroughly confuse them. How could the man who owned the threshing machine allow a combine on his farm? Fortunately, none came by while Olson was in the clover field, and at day's end, Pa had several big, canvas grain bags filled with red clover seed. Total cost for combining: $6.50.

The cost to hull clover with a stationary clover huller would be about the same. The big difference was the amount of labor involved. With the stationary machine, the clover would have to be cut with a mower, raked, bunched, and then hauled some distance to the huller. This job was something like threshing day in miniature—not as many men, say a half dozen or so. But with the combine, one man could do it all.

A few years later, the Macijeski brothers, whose farm abutted ours on the east, bought a new John Deere combine. That signaled the beginning of the end for threshing in our community.

Within half a dozen years, all the farmers in our neighborhood had abandoned the grain binder and the thresher in favor of the combine. Farmers, when they gathered at Hotz's or the gristmill or a tavern, sometimes looked back on the old days of threshing and compared it with the advantages and disadvantages of combining.

They talked about the amount of straw the combine left in the field, and compared it with the big stacks of straw the threshing machine used to produce. More farmers were now forced to buy straw, and the stacks that once rose up behind neighborhood barns every August were no more.

On the other hand, no one missed steering a grain binder around an oat field on a hot day, especially when a fickle knotter jammed or simply refused to tie knots and spewed loose oat bundles. No one missed shocking grain either. This job was even worse than bunching hay, which at least involved a pitchfork. When you shocked grain, you picked up every bundle by hand. First you tucked one bundle under each arm, then you stood the pair in place. Five or six pairs of bundles made a shock. If Canada thistles grew in the grain-field hollows, the dry thistles perforated your shirt and tore at your sweaty arms.

But our neighborhood lost something important when combines replaced the threshing machine. We lost the gatherings of farmers to share work and joke and tell stories and eat grand meals. Threshing had been more than harvesting grain; it had been a social event, where boys demonstrated they were becoming men, where farmers boasted about whose tractor was best, where farmwives competed to make the best apple pie and the fluffiest mashed potatoes. I remember those threshing dinners fondly, the thickly sliced roast beef, huge bowls of potatoes, a gravy boat filled with rich brown gravy, a stack of bread that disappeared nearly as quickly as it appeared on the table, and bowls of mixed vegetables—peas, carrots, baby onions. And the pies, who could forget the apple, peach, cherry, wild raspberry, or blueberry pies? It was a banquet for a bunch of dirty, smelly, storytelling men.

Combines changed all of this. They not only changed how farmers harvested grain, they changed the social interaction in rural communities. And for young guys like me, they changed how we demonstrated that we had become men.

CHAPTER 22

⌇

Fire

Fire loss—$300.00
Fire insurance payment—$110.00

During an afternoon recess, my classmates and I were in the
schoolyard playing softball. It was September, the weather was
pleasantly warm, and the sky was the bluest it had been for days. A
slight breeze blew from the southwest. The five-leafed woodbine
growing on the schoolyard fence had recently turned a brilliant
red, the maples to the west showed orange, and the early golden-
rods in the field to the south were the deepest, most brilliant
yellow I had ever seen.

"Wonder why all those cars are going up Miller's Hill?" Jim
Kolka asked. Miller's Hill ran north of the school. We walked it
every day to and from school.

We stopped playing ball and watched a string of cars head
up the long hill, stirring up dust that drifted off to the east. Ordinarily, no more than a handful of cars drove up Miller's Hill on
any given day: the mailman, a neighbor hauling grist to the mill,
maybe the Watkins man peddling his wares. Never before had I
seen so many cars on Miller's Hill and driving fast, too—as fast
as cars can climb a steep hill on a dirt road. Something unusual
was happening, something very unusual.

Then we spotted Elsie Jenks, who lived less than a quarter mile east of the school, hurrying toward us. She entered the schoolyard out of breath.

"Jerry, it's you I'm looking for." She paused to catch her breath. "Just had a general ring on the telephone that your barn is on fire."

It was like someone had hit me in the stomach. "Thank you," I muttered. "Thank you for telling me."

"Your ma just called, too. She said you should stay at school with your brothers, that you'd be safer here."

I felt like crying. Felt like I should run home as fast as I could and help Pa. Now I knew why the cars were speeding up Miller's Hill; they were on their way to try to save our barn. I also knew that once a barn caught fire, no matter how many neighbors turned out, the building usually burned to the ground, especially if it was as full of hay as was ours. The best the neighbors could generally do was douse the other buildings with pails of water—if they had enough—to keep the fire from burning everything. In those days, the sole fire truck in Wild Rose stayed in Wild Rose. It never traveled outside the village, no matter how serious the fire. Fighting fire was a neighborhood's responsibility, and most neighborhoods had no firefighting equipment, not even a fire extinguisher.

The afternoon dragged on unmercifully slowly. I didn't want to be in school. I belonged at home. I looked over at my brothers, who sat across the room. I could see tears in their eyes.

Farm kids knew the dangers of fire and especially the devastation caused by a barn fire. Barns were virtual tinderboxes, with all the flammable hay and straw and the wooden construction. A tipped-over kerosene lantern, a load of insufficiently dried hay— these things could easily spark a fire or spontaneously combust. Most of us had witnessed at least one barn fire. A couple years earlier, I had seen the one that burned Alfred Jenks's barn. Pa and I arrived when most of the building had already collapsed on top of the cows. The men who arrived first on the scene told us how they had tried to remove the cows but the flames were too intense. They watched and listened to the awful cries of the cattle as they died in the holocaust.

Finally, four o'clock arrived and my brothers and I hurried up Miller's Hill, not knowing what to expect at home. By the time we crested the hill, a thread of black smoke rose in the distance. I feared the worst. We continued past Miller's farm and on to our place. As we neared our farm, cars lined both sides of the road all the way to our driveway and beyond. We rushed up the driveway.

I couldn't believe what I saw. Our barn was still standing, though badly charred. So was the red wooden silo next to it and the pump house a few hundred feet away. The elevated water pipes, which formerly connected the pump house to the barn, lay on the ground in a grotesque tangle of bent metal.

Our dooryard was filled with what looked like several hundred people. In the middle of the barnyard was a heap of smoking, smoldering straw—what remained of our once magnificent straw stack. We had threshed only a few days earlier and put up one of our largest stacks ever. Soot-covered men continued to toss water on the south side of the once-white pump house; the water turned to steam when it struck the still-hot building. Other men tossed pails of water on the silo and the barn, to prevent the wood from reigniting.

I saw Pa standing near the smoldering straw stack. His face was blackened with soot and streaked with sweat. I asked him what had happened.

"A stranger driving by this afternoon saw smoke coming from the straw stack. He stopped and told us," Pa said quietly. He looked exhausted. "I didn't believe him. Thought he must be seeing things. And then I looked, and by God, he was right, there was smoke coming from the straw stack. Wasn't any fire yet, just smoke pouring out the top of the stack."

Later, Pa surmised that spontaneous combustion had set the straw stack ablaze. Every year before threshing season, Pa built a little wooden structure to shelter our heifers in the winter. He would cover it with fresh hay and then, when we threshed, bury the shelter under the straw stack. After threshing season, we would dig through the straw to the shelter, making a tunnel for the heifers. In previous years, the buried shelter had kept the heifers warm and comfortable. This year, the hay must not have been dry enough when we heaped straw on the shelter. Damp hay compressed into an airless space—whether in a hayloft or under a straw stack—could spontaneously combust; this was the cause of many barn fires.

Pa went on with the story. "Once we saw the smoke, Ma got on the phone with a general ring and people started coming from every direction. Never saw so many people. They brought milk pails and milk cans filled with water from their stock tanks. Everybody knew there was never enough water at a fire."

Pa stopped to draw a soot-covered handkerchief from his pocket and swab it across his sweating forehead.

"Stack was still smoking when the first people arrived, and then with a *swoosh* the fire broke out the top, and we were in trouble. Thought for sure we'd lose the barn. Several men crawled up on the barn roof and, with a bucket brigade, poured water down the roof and the sides of the building. Another guy—never saw him before—climbed on top of the silo, and men began passing buckets of water to him, which he poured down the smoking sides. Smoke was so thick sometimes you couldn't even make out this guy, but he stayed there and saved the silo.

"Danny Macijeski said that we were never gonna save the barn or the silo without moving the burning straw stack. I didn't know how he was gonna do that. But he and Bill Miller pulled loose the steel cable from our manure carrier and wrapped it around the bottom of the stack—the fire was still only on the top. Danny hooked his B to one end of the cable and I hooked our H to the other and we pulled the burning straw stack out here in the middle of the barnyard. It was one hot tractor pull, and I worried that hunks of burning straw would land on Danny or me, but they didn't.

"Had to keep pouring water on all the buildings, though. Porch roof on the house caught fire once when a chunk of burning straw landed on it. Got it out before it did any damage."

Someone wanted to show Pa something and he hurried off, leaving me to think about the disaster that had been averted. I silently thanked the huge number of people who had dropped what they were doing and hurried to our farm. Their quick thinking likely saved our barn, our silo, our pump house, and probably our farmhouse as well. The side of the silo continued to steam, as did the barn siding, but the fire was clearly out. Just the remnants of the straw stack still quietly burned in the barnyard, a couple of men watching it so it wouldn't once more spread.

Soot-covered men began gathering up their milk pails and milk cans. Some looked out from almost completely black faces, but they were all smiling. At least this once, they had saved a barn. To a person, they were proud. Very proud.

Pa walked from person to person, shaking hands and thanking each one.

CHAPTER 23

~🙦~

Silo Filling

Filling silo (Ross Caves)—$14.00

In mid-September, Pa walked the twenty-acre cornfield south of
the barn daily. He was checking whether the corn was ready to
put in the silo. To the untrained eye, the green kernels seemed
a long way from maturity, but good corn silage—what resulted
after the corn in the silo fermented—required green corn. Pa
was watching for the kernels to mature to the "milk stage." You
could tell the corn was ready when you squished a kernel and it
squirted white liquid.

Once Pa determined it was time, he called Ross Caves in Wild
Rose, who owned a silo filler. Pa scheduled a day for Ross to bring
his machine to the farm, then contacted our neighbors, who traveled as a crew from farm to farm, helping fill silos. Pa and I would
cut the corn ourselves with the corn binder. The crew would show
up the next day, ready to haul bundled corn while Ross operated
the silo filler. We needed to fill the silo the day after cutting the
corn, while it was still green and full of moisture.

After Pa made his calls, we were off to the cornfield, me with
the corn knife, and Pa with Frank and Charlie, our draft horses,
hitched to the McCormick-Deering corn binder. Someone had

to cut a corn row by hand to make room for the team and the machine. Farmers planted rows three and a half feet apart in those days, so cutting one row resulted in a seven-foot corridor. I sometimes did the hand cutting, though Pa did for a while, concluding that I was too slow or too inept. I tried to keep up this image as long as I could, but Pa, being uncommonly bright about such matters, soon figured it out, and I was out there swinging the corn knife, inept or not.

A corn knife consists of a curved blade attached to a two-foot-long hickory handle. You held a corn stalk in one hand, the knife in the other hand, and then you whacked the stalk off. It was all manpower—no machines, no horses—just you, the corn knife, and the corn, sweat running down your face and corn leaves scratching your arms.

After a row was cut, Pa maneuvered the corn binder down the open corridor. The machine had two snouts that moved on each side of a corn row. A short, sharp sickle severed each corn plant. The corn then fell into a device that gathered the stalks into a bundle, wrapped the bundle with twine, and dropped the bound bundle to the ground. Pa knew from experience how many rows of corn would fill our silo; he was usually accurate within a wagonload or two. The corn binder operated many times faster than cutting corn by hand, and, of course, the process was much easier because you only needed to steer the team down the rows. The binder even had a seat. If you didn't mind the rumble and shaking, you could ride. Or you could walk behind.

In the evening after a day of cutting corn, Ross came with his silo filler and set it up outside our red wooden silo. We bolted together various lengths of silo-filler pipe, extending the pipe from the filler to a little window at the top of the silo. To open the window, someone had to climb the wobbly ladder attached to the outside of the silo, hanging on with one hand and opening the window with the other. Duck usually got this job. He enjoyed

gazing all around the neighborhood. The one time I crawled up
the ladder, I was so afraid of falling, I couldn't do anything except
shakily climb back down, wringing wet with sweat.

With the corn cut and bound in the field, and the silo filler set
up, all was in readiness. Our neighbors arrived the next morning,
three with their teams and wagons, plus a couple more to help
load bundles in the field. Soon, the first wagonload of green corn
stalks pulled up to the filler. Ross brought his Farmall M tractor
up to speed and the filler began its high-pitched whine. Men fed
cornstalk bundles onto the conveyor. In turn, the conveyor pulled
the corn into the machine's knives, which sliced the stalks into
half-inch pieces, and then into the blower, which sent the pieces
flying up the pipe and into the empty silo.

Pa and I usually worked inside the silo, packing down the
corn pieces that flew in through the silo window. We crawled up
the silo chute, an enclosed ladder on the barn side of the silo. I
didn't fear heights if I couldn't see off in the distance. The sound
in the silo was akin to being inside a metal-roofed barn during a
hailstorm, times three. But the freshly cut corn smelled pleasant
and earthy, and the material squished as we walked around and
around inside the silo, packing down the silage.

By noon, the silo was half full. The men filed into the farmhouse, tossing their hats in a corner of the porch before pulling
open the screen door. There was the usual joshing, joke telling,
and tractor comparing. The discussion usually came down to
which was better: a John Deere B or a Farmall H tractor. The
same discussion came up whenever the neighbors gathered, and
the end result was usually a tie: the B is best, the H is best.

In the dining room, Ma had pulled the oak table to its greatest
extension with all the extra table boards. Aunt Louise had come
out from town to help Ma prepare the meal. Ma had started the
day before by baking bread and pies and had gotten up before
dawn today to fire up the cookstove, peel potatoes and carrots,

and start the roast beef. The crew that sat down to the table was sweaty, dirty, and hungry. Pa and I sat down last, but even though I was only fourteen, I was doing a man's work in the field, and was thus entitled to eat with the men.

By the time the last man took his chair, Ma and Aunt Louise had spread the long table with platters of roast beef, bowls of mashed potatoes with huge hunks of butter floating on top, bowls of carrots, plates of dill pickles, two gravy boats filled just short of spilling out their spouts, and two plates stacked high with fresh bread, one huge plate for each end of the table. The plates and platters emptied as the men passed the dishes. Ma and Louise quickly refilled.

For the first few minutes of the meal, a great quiet came over the sweat-stained farmers. But then, as the first pangs of hunger were satisfied, the banter began again.

"Pitiful-looking corn crop you got this year, Bill. Looks like you'll have to cut her with a grain binder it looks so short." And then raucous laughter because everyone knew Bill's corn was as good as anyone else's.

Soon, Ma and Aunt Louise brought the pies—cherry, apple, peach—from the kitchen, each cut in five pieces. Most men took at least two pieces; some took three pieces, one of each kind.

The coffee was passed, and passed again, as the men washed down the enormous meal. A huge gray coffeepot stood on the back of the woodstove, ready to provide refills.

And then it was over. What had taken Ma hours to prepare disappeared in minutes. The men slowly moved outside, retrieved their hats from the porch, and gathered under the big elm tree not far from the kitchen door. They continued the debate over which was the best model tractor, with someone suggesting they should throw Case, Oliver, and Allis-Chalmers into the mix.

Soon the men headed back to the cornfield and the filling continued. By five o'clock, the silo was filled nearly to the top.

Pa and I had removed all the distribution pipes and sent them down the silo chute.

Now the bare, curved end of the filler blower pipe confronted us. We no longer had room to stand, and we worked on our hands and knees. Cut corn hit us in the face, pelting us in the back when we turned. It was like being in a hailstorm. We pushed the corn into every corner under the silo roof, moving it with our hands, packing it with our knees. Soon our heads were bumping against the roof. And the corn kept coming, kept trying to bury me as I pushed the material away until there was no place to push it. I started to feel frantic.

"I'm being buried," I yelled. "I'm being buried!"

Pa said nothing, just kept pushing silage out of the way. I don't know if he didn't hear or simply ignored me. I thought we were doomed.

Suddenly, Pa pushed a handful of cut corn out the silo window, and everything stopped. Outside, the whine of the tractor ceased. Without a word, Pa crawled down the silo chute, and I followed.

The men filed into the house for the evening meal—not as expansive as the noon meal, but substantial. Aunt Louise stayed on through the afternoon, helping prepare supper. Once again the tired, sweaty men found their places at the dining room table and feasted on fried potatoes, boiled ring bologna, coleslaw, home-canned peas, bowls of applesauce, and immense pieces of German chocolate cake with quarter-inch-high chocolate frosting. Cups of black coffee topped off the meal. The talk around the table was about the day and how well it had gone, and a hope that the weather would hold so Bill Miller could fill his silo the next day. All the men had chores to do at home, so when they pushed back their chairs from the near-empty table, they departed. As each neighbor left, Pa thanked him and said he looked forward to filling silo at his place.

Overnight, the cut corn settled several feet. The next morning, a couple neighbors returned and again filled the silo to the top. Pa and I once more crawled up the silo chute and pushed and packed the new offering of cut corn. But first Ross started the filler and blew fresh air into the silo. Silo gas, a deadly mixture of nitrogen dioxide and carbon dioxide formed when the corn fermented, killed several farmers every year. Running the filler for a few minutes drove off any gas that may have developed.

In October, we began feeding the cows corn silage. One of my chores was to climb up the silo chute, open a wooden door, and pitch out the silage. The once-green corn had turned a reddish brown and smelled slightly acidic. Our cows relished corn silage. At one time, some farmers dismissed silage as a fad, causing some cheese factories to refuse milk from silage-fed cows. No more. Silage had become a mainstay winter feed.

The following year at the Waushara County Fair, Pa and I inspected the new farm machinery, as we did every year. We saw a machine that looked like a cross between a corn binder and a silo filler.

"It's a forage harvester," the salesman said. "You pull it with your tractor, and it not only cuts the corn stalks, it slices them into little pieces and blows them into a wagon you pull along behind."

He showed us the wagon and its unloading device. Once you had a wagonload of cut corn, he explained, it was mechanically unloaded into a blower that sent it up into your silo. The machine cost about a thousand dollars.

"Don't expect we'll be able to afford something like that," Pa said. "Especially when it takes only a couple, three days to fill the silo by ourselves, without needing the neighbors to help."

The forage harvester took away most of the manual labor involved in silo filling. It eliminated the corn binder, corn bundles, and the need to haul them to a silo filler. The silo filler itself was replaced with a simpler machine that had only to blow the cut corn into the silo. A farmer could do the entire job by himself, filling his silo in a day or so, depending on the quality of the corn and the size of the silo.

Pa and I didn't know that the forage harvester signaled the end of the silo filling crew that once made its way around the neighborhood. Filling silo was much more than helping a neighbor with work he couldn't do alone. It was a way for neighbors to get together, to share stories, to jibe each other about the superiority of their tractors, and to taste the cooking of the neighborhood women and quietly compare notes. In our neighborhood—with its mixture of German, Norwegian, Polish, Bohemian, Welsh, and English families—the foods served were as diverse as the ethnic roots of the farmers. When the forage harvester appeared, all of this disappeared.

Though Pa never purchased the expensive machine, several of our neighbors did. By the mid-1950s, Pa was forced to buy a used silo filler so we could fill our silo on our own. He still used a corn binder, except now it was pulled by a tractor. And I still had to cut a row or two of corn every year with the dreaded corn knife.

CHAPTER 24

꜆

Shredding Corn

Shredding corn (Vilas Olson)—$46.00

In October, a month after filling the silo with cut green corn, we harvested the rest of our cornfield for the mature ears and the dried cornstalks. Throughout the late 1930s and 1940s, all the farmers in central Wisconsin cut and bound their corn with one-row horse-drawn corn binders. That is, all except Albert Davis and his bachelor son, Bernard.

Albert and Bernard cut their corn by hand, with corn knives. They bound the bundles by hand, too. Then they stood the bundles in corn shocks and left the shocks to dry through the fall and into early winter. When the corn had thoroughly dried, they'd hitch their team of skinny horses to a wagon, drive to the cornfield, and load a few shocks of corn. If the snow was deep, they'd shovel out the shocks and sometimes use axes to chop ice that had accumulated at the bottom of the stalks. The process was slow, tedious, and cold. Then they hauled the corn bundles to the open area between the haymows in their barn, once called the threshing floor, and spent their winter days husking corn by hand, one cob at a time. Farmers had harvested corn this way since the days of Thomas Jefferson and George Washington.

Albert and Bernard provided a valuable model for our neighborhood, especially for the young people. None of us, no matter
what, wanted to end up like Bernard Davis.

In comparison, the way my family harvested corn seemed
considerably advanced. We cut and bound our corn with a corn
binder, at first horse-drawn and later pulled by our Farmall H
tractor. We did shock the corn by hand. But on a cool autumn
day, when the trees were a rainbow of colors and skeins of geese
flew overhead, it was not an unpleasant job. Besides, you could
see the results of your efforts in the corn shocks marching across
the cornfield at day's end.

Come November, Vilas Olson, who owned a corn shredder,
began making the rounds of the neighborhood. His corn shredder mechanically husked the corn and shredded the stalks. Like
the threshing crews of August, corn shredding was another community event, although the weather was much colder and more
disagreeable and men worked hard to finish the job or just to
keep warm.

On corn-shredding day, three or four neighbors drove their
teams to the cornfield, tore apart the corn shocks, and loaded
the corn bundles on a wagon. At the shredder, the men hand-fed
bundles into the machine, one bundle at a time. On our farm, we
blew the shredded stalks into the upper barn; we'd later use the
material for cow feed and bedding. The husked corn ears traveled
up a little conveyor and tumbled into a wagon. When the wagon
was full, we shoveled the corn into our corncrib. Later, we would
grind the corncobs at the gristmill in Wild Rose and mix them
with oats to use as cattle feed throughout the winter.

One day's work with the corn shredder resulted in more corn
husked than Albert and Bernard could accomplish all winter
doing it by hand on their cold and drafty threshing floor. The
hungry shredding crew often talked about Albert and Bernard
at the dinner and supper table. We poked fun at their primitive

harvesting approach. Some of the older men in the crew recalled the days before machines when they, too, husked corn by hand. There is little excitement connected to husking by hand, one cob at a time, hour upon hour, on a cold, drafty barn floor. It may have given Bernard and his father something to do on long, gloomy winter days, but they missed out on the gatherings of men who formed the corn-shredding crews that moved from farm to farm, eating thresher-style meals, sharing stories, and pulling pranks.

Little did we know that, by the mid-1950s, our "advanced" corn binders and shredders would be left behind as well. Our neighbor to the east, Danny Macijeski, was the first to buy a tractor-operated mechanical corn picker. This machine traveled down the cornrows, husking corn and dumping the ears into a wagon pulled behind. No corn cutting with a binder. No shocking by hand. No shredding crew coming to your farm.

The corn picker meant farmers could now harvest their corn without their neighbors' help. Strange as it might seem, from a social perspective, what Albert and Bernard had been doing all along on their threshing floor is what the rest of the farmers did now, albeit with expensive new harvesting equipment. They worked by themselves, in isolation.

The corn picker took another step toward the time when farmers would leave the land by the thousands, because a machine now did the work of several men.

CHAPTER 25

～

Windstorm

Insurance for barn—$1,993.89
Government indemnity—$100.00 per cow

In the spring of 1950, a string of warm days stretched from late April into May. The oat crop was coming up, the cornfield was mostly plowed, and the pastureland was beginning to turn green.

Red tinged the eastern sky as I hustled to the barn for the morning milking. It was awesomely quiet, no birds singing, no ruffed grouse drumming in the woods, not even a crow cawing.

Pa was busy milking when I arrived in the barn.

"Strange morning," I said.

"Storm comin'," he replied.

Frank and Charlie were uneasy in their stalls, swishing their tails and stamping their hoofs. Our big Holstein herd bull, confined in his reinforced stall, made a low guttural sound that he sometimes made when he was upset. Fanny lay quietly behind the cows, head resting on her paws, as if waiting for something. The barn cats clustered around their milk dish, waiting for their morning handout. The milk cows seemed edgy and uneasy, rattling the stanchions that confined them and occasionally mooing. Something was going to happen.

By late morning, the wind had picked up from the southwest. By noon, straw from the mostly used up straw stack swirled around the yard and blew between the house and barn. A dead branch on the box elder tree near the chicken house crashed to the ground. By suppertime, the wind roared like a hundred-car freight train. Yellowish-brown dust boiled up from the recently planted oat fields, tearing out the new oat plants. Dust, straw, twigs—the clutter that accumulates from a long winter—filled the sky. The sun was scarcely visible behind a sickly yellow veil.

"Hope the wind goes down tonight," Pa said during the evening milking. "Starting to do a lot of damage to the oat fields."

After milking, I crawled up the ladder into the haymow to toss down hay for the cows. I was immediately confronted with the sounds of the barn protesting the storm. The beams creaked, the big haymow doors clattered and banged, a loose outside board pounded like a hammer. The wind screaming around the corners and over the roof nearly silenced the other sounds of complaint. I thought I could feel the mostly empty haymow shudder against the gusting wind. But I figured it was my imagination.

Pa and I braced ourselves against the wind as we hurried back to the farmhouse. In the kitchen, Ma was complaining about the wind. Her wood-burning kitchen stove had been smoking so bad she had to let it go out. The cookstove sometimes smoked, but never so much Ma couldn't use it.

The wind didn't die down that night. When my brothers and I went to bed, it was whistling around the house and rattling our bedroom windows. If anything, the wind was growing stronger.

I awoke in the dim light of dawn to my mother screaming, "The barn is going over! The barn is going over!"

My brothers and I leaped out of bed and pulled on our clothes as we ran along the hall and down the stairway. In the dining room, Ma was on the telephone, ringing a series of short rings and then shouting into the mouthpiece.

My brothers and I ran outside. The relentless west wind shrieked and the air still swirled with flying straw, dust, broken twigs, and pine needles. Through the clutter, the barn still seemed to be standing. We raced across the yard, and I yanked open the barn door. Inside was bedlam. The barn teetered on its foundation. Huge wooden beams had fallen across the cattle and across the horse stalls. Cows lay pinned under the beams, bawling in pain. The horses dug their hoofs into the floorboards, trying and failing to stand under the heavy beams. The herd bull, standing on a pile of broken wall blocks, bellowed in a way I had never heard. Above all the cries, the wind howled and shook the barn without mercy.

Pa stood in the middle of it all, struggling to pull a beam off the cattle. "Help me with this beam," he yelled. His face was red, his wire-rimmed glasses askew, and his false teeth gagging him.

The solid oak beam that formerly supported the upper part of the barn measured some thirty feet long and at least ten-by-ten inches. Together, the four of us managed to lift it off the cattle. A few cows struggled to their feet. I ran in front of them, opening their stanchions, while Pa strained to open the door to the barnyard.

We herded the cows toward the door and safety. Those that could still walk climbed over the clutter of broken boards and wall masonry, but not without considerable encouragement. They knew the barn as a safe place and wanted to remain there. But the barn balanced on a single section of wall that remained standing and could topple the rest of the way any minute.

I ran to the calf pen and found several calves buried in the rubble, two already dead. Another had a broken, twisted leg; two others were scratched and scraped. My 4-H calf lay buried up to its head. I frantically dug away the clutter and carried him outside, then returned to help with the other three surviving calves.

Pa turned the horses out. Miraculously, they were only slightly injured. He also untied the herd bull, which followed Pa out like a kitten on a string. Pa chained the huge animal to a post near the straw stack, and we continued to herd out the remaining cows.

We returned to the interior of the barn again and again. None of us thought much about the dangerous situation—how the barn might fall on us any minute, trapping us like it had the livestock.

By this time, neighbors were arriving, carloads of them. John Macijeski took charge of stabilizing the barn, instructing men where to carry wooden blocks that were left from when we moved the barn a few years earlier. Now the blocks provided a temporary foundation so the barn wouldn't topple.

Shortly after sunrise, the wind began to die, and by noon, it was no more than a stiff breeze that blew cold from the northwest. The men managed to stabilize the barn, but it had shifted six feet or more to the east, tipping the east wall and toppling the west wall altogether.

All the cows could walk, though several limped severely and a couple bore cuts on their backs where the beam had landed. The herd bull had cut and bruised legs, but he seemed otherwise unharmed. The horses stood in the corner of the barnyard, uninjured.

The immediate problem was finding shelter for the cows and a place to milk them. We'd missed the morning milking and needed to milk them in the afternoon. Meanwhile, our neighbors fixed a temporary calf pen in the tractor shed; the calves would be comfortable there. The bull could stay outside for the short term, as could the horses. But we needed something more permanent for the cattle.

Paul Krueger, a cattle dealer who lived about three miles east on County A, offered to take in our cows. He had a sizable barn on his farm, and he could house them until a barn mover, stone masons, and carpenters put our barn back in order.

Pa gratefully accepted Krueger's offer. Around noon, several of us—some neighbors, Pa, my brothers, and I—drove the cattle the mile south to the county road and then two more miles east. We moved slowly, stopping often to rest the limping cattle. The entire herd was upset. Some did not want to be driven and continually turned around, trying to head home. By mid-afternoon, we arrived at Krueger's farm and herded the cattle into the barnyard.

We spent a couple hours sweeping and trying to make the seldom-used barn comfortable for our agitated cattle. We moved them into stalls, and by late afternoon, we were milking—by hand, as Krueger had no milking machine. We scarcely had time to consider the immensity of our loss. For a dairy farmer, all activity centers on the barn. It houses the primary source of income, the milk cows, and it provides a storage place for hay. A barn is where a dairy farmer spends several hours each day, all year long. Now our barn was unusable.

That entire summer, we drove to Krueger's farm twice a day to milk our fifteen-cow herd by hand. They subsisted on dry hay, and milk production went down. Pa hired a contractor, Mr. Rasmusen, and a barn-moving crew arrived within a week of the windstorm. In a few short days, they had the barn back to its original position. But the rest of the summer passed as masons built new walls and a crew of carpenters put beams and boards back in place. Haying season arrived, and without a usable hayloft, we were forced to make huge haystacks outside. No matter how well you constructed a haystack, or how carefully you covered the top with strips of roofing paper, the weather spoiled a considerable quantity of hay in an outdoor stack. To have good hay, it must be stored indoors.

The crew finished work in late summer. We drove the herd back home, where the cows could return to our alfalfa pastures and, we hoped, milk production would return to pre-windstorm levels. The repaired barn smelled fresh and clean. The milking machine made a welcome sound, though some of the cows had difficulty readjusting to the machine after months of being milked by hand. The insurance check arrived: $1,993.89. Pa signed the entire amount over to Rasmusen. The rest of the costs, several hundred dollars, Pa paid himself, wiping out much of his meager savings.

But with the cattle back, we all breathed a sigh of relief. At least now, we felt farm life would return to some semblance of normalcy. How wrong we were.

In those years, brucellosis—commonly called Bang's disease— was ravaging Midwestern dairy herds. A cow would appear normal, but she would abort her calf long before it was due. Even worse, her milk was contaminated and caused a disease, called undulant fever, in people. The state agricultural departments were frantic, until scientists discovered a blood test that detected the disease, and created a vaccine that prevented it in young animals. We had our calves vaccinated, as required by the state, and our cows were tested regularly.

Late that summer, after a routine test, all our cows except one tested positive for brucellosis. The law said they must be slaughtered. The state would provide an indemnity of one hundred dollars for each cow, to partially cover the animal's value.

Fourteen of our fifteen cows had to be destroyed. We had known these cows since they were calves. They had names— Mary, Jane, Eleanor, Sady, Lorraine, Mildred. They had personalities, special traits, likes and dislikes. We knew each one as a member of the family, as indeed they were. Now they had to be destroyed, all except Violet, who for some reason tested negative and continued to do so each time she was tested.

Ross Caves, the local trucker, sent two cattle trucks to our farm on a Monday morning in September. Each cow walked up the ramp into the truck. They looked at us through the slats, wondering what now, after all they had been through that summer. It was a sadder morning than when the barn nearly blew over. It was one of the few times I ever saw Pa cry, as his prized possessions walked up the ramp to their slaughter.

The freshly repaired barn was eerily quiet. The occupants included the herd bull, a pen full of healthy calves, the team of horses, and Violet, standing alone with empty stalls on either side. Our future dairy herd was jumping around in the calf pen. In the meantime, Pa needed replacement cows.

The next day, Pa went looking for cattle, with the $1,400 from the government. He found a swayback Holstein, a couple Guernseys, a few skinny Holsteins, and a Jersey-Holstein cross that was the homeliest critter to ever set foot on the farm. I suspect Pa would like to have hidden them in the back pasture, they made such an unremarkable herd. Our motley new cows could not match the milk production of our former prized herd, but we were dairy farmers, and dairy farmers must have milk cows.

Pa often remarked after that summer how one disaster can result in another, sometimes worse, disaster. Paul Krueger's barn had been infected by brucellosis-carrying animals before we ever housed our herd there. If only we had known, but Krueger himself had no idea his barn, standing straight and true, was a time bomb for disaster.

Economic conditions had always been difficult on our farm. But in the years following the windstorm, times were as difficult as they had ever been, including throughout the Great Depression. For the next few summers, Pa planted more cucumbers and green beans—up to five acres each, instead of one or two—and expanded the strawberry patch. We needed the extra income as we waited for the dairy herd to return to full production. This meant everyone worked harder and for less overall income. There was little complaining about the hard work or reduced income. Without saying anything, Pa convinced me and my brothers, through his actions, that the family had to work together as a team if we were to survive these hard times. Each of us, without bragging or talking about it, was proud to help; each of us knew our contribution was important to the farm's survival. Those years brought our family as close together as it had ever been.

In the wake of the windstorm, I learned that a seemingly isolated event can have effects that go on for years. A windstorm that lasted less than twenty-four hours affected my family economically for five years—and emotionally, for untold years.

CHAPTER 26

~

New Neighbor

Witt farm—$5,000.00

George Luedtke knew nothing about practical farming. But he thought he did. After all, he had read every book and magazine article about agriculture he could find in the year before he moved to our neighborhood.

Luedtke grew up in Milwaukee, and he had always wanted to live in the country. Throughout World War II, he worked for A. O. Smith, a Milwaukee company actively involved in making war materiel. With the war over, he had saved enough money that, together with the sale of his house, he could buy a farm. He and his wife, Ruth, and their two little boys, Johnny and David, looked forward to moving away from the noisy, smelly city to the quiet life of the farm. They had no idea what they were getting into.

The farm the Luedtkes picked was my grandpa Witt's old farm, a mile west of our place. Pa had been trying to sell the place for several years, ever since my grandparents' death in 1941. Selling during the war proved impossible. Pa found renters for a time, but none stayed, and we farmed both our place and the Witt farm for several years.

With the war ended, Pa advertised the farm again, and George Luedtke wrote to say he was interested. After an exchange of letters, the Luedtkes arrived for a look around. George was tall, pale after working years inside, and thin to the point of frailty. His little brown moustache jerked up and down when he talked. No one in our neighborhood wore a moustache or a beard, so that single feature set him apart. As it turned out, he differed from the neighbors in many ways beyond a moustache.

The Luedtkes apparently liked what they saw during their visit. In a few weeks, they closed the deal and paid Pa cash. This was most unusual. Nearly every farmer in our neighborhood had taken out a mortgage when he first bought his farm; some still had a mortgage, although higher farm income during the war helped many farmers pay off their debt.

Luedtke asked Pa if he would help him get started farming. Pa smiled and said, "Sure, just ask me what you'd like to know." Luedtke knew so little about practical farming he didn't know what to ask. He bought a herd of skinny dairy cows from an old farmer who quickly figured out Luedtke was a greenhorn and didn't know a cow's udder from its tail. When Pa saw the sorry collection of cows, he mentioned to Luedtke that maybe he, Pa, could have helped pick out the cows.

"Didn't need help with buying cows," Luedtke said. "Read about it. Read about what makes a good cow."

He apparently hadn't read enough or the right material. These homely cows looked like their milk would scarcely cover the bottom of a milk pail. For several of the skinniest cows, standing up and chewing their cuds appeared a challenge.

"You know how to milk?" Pa asked.

"Here's where I need some help," Luedtke admitted. "Couldn't find anything in my books about how to milk a cow." He fooled with his mustache when he talked.

That evening, Pa sent me over to show our new neighbor how to milk. I demonstrated how to hold a milk pail between your legs while balancing on a three-legged milk stool. I showed Luedtke how to tuck the cow's tail under your knee so she couldn't whop you in the face. Then I grabbed a teat in each hand, squeezed and pulled, and a stream of fresh milk zinged against the pail. Soon, a layer of milk covered the bottom of the pail.

"Your turn," I said. I was in eighth grade and feeling cocky that I knew how to do something an adult didn't, even if he was only a city guy.

"Looks easy enough," Luedtke said.

I got up from under the cow and handed over the pail and stool. He sat down and struggled to hold the pail between his legs while also tucking the cow's tail under his knee. I said to forget about the tail for the time being.

Luedtke grabbed hold of the cow's teats and gave a mighty tug to both at the same time. The cow looked around to see what strange creature was mauling her and shuffled her back legs back and forth.

"Stand still," Luedtke said loudly. He gave another a mighty tug, but no milk zinged into the pail, not a drop.

"What's wrong here?" he asked. "You got milk; I'm not getting any milk."

"Let me show you again." I leaned over his shoulder, grabbed one of the teats, and squeezed and gently pulled. A fat stream of milk shot into the pail.

"How'd you do that?"

"Let me show you again." I repeated the demonstration.

Luedtke grabbed hold of both teats again and gave a mighty pull. The cow lifted one of her hind feet and planted it squarely on Luedtke's foot. At the same time, she slapped him across the face with her wiry tail.

Luedtke jerked loose his foot, dumping the pail and over-turning the stool. "Stupid beast!" he yelled. He jumped up and down behind the cow. "Stupid beast!" His face was red, his mustache bobbed up and down, and perspiration dripped from his forehead.

"Look at this, will you?" He showed me his hand, which had swollen to the size of a balloon. Later, I learned that he had squeezed the teat so hard he had broken a blood vessel in his hand.

Pa made a deal with Luedtke that I would spend the week living with the Luedtke family to teach George how to milk. At the end of the week, he bought a milking machine and I went home. I doubt he ever learned how to milk by hand.

A couple weeks later, Luedtke stopped by the farm and left a small package for me. It was a book, Horace Kephart's *Camping and Woodcraft*. Luedtke knew of my interest in the outdoors, and he couldn't have given me a finer present. I have the book in my library to this day, and whenever I pick it up, I'm reminded of my week trying to teach our new neighbor how to milk. As a teacher, I had been a miserable failure.

Slowly, our community accepted the Luedtke family, not because George Luedtke became a good farmer. He didn't. But the Luedtkes were good, honest people, and they involved themselves in community activities.

George became clerk of the Chain O' Lake school board. He organized a community drama club and put on plays at the country schoolhouse. Most of the adults in our community hadn't graduated eighth grade, and none of this new cadre of "actors" had ever been onstage. George Luedtke convinced old and young alike that they could recite lines, sing songs, entertain the rest of the community, and have a good time doing it.

The drama club performed for about four years, doing mostly comedies that appealed to young and old. Luedtke and Faith Jenks selected the plays and picked actors for the various roles. Show nights filled the little one-room schoolhouse. Some spectators came to see their neighbors "make fools of themselves." But most attended because they knew they would have a good time, and almost always, they did. Seeing a neighbor flub his lines was as much fun as seeing one perform well.

Luedtke was well-read, with an urban perspective to be sure, but he achieved the seemingly impossible—helping people get out of their individual worlds. For the young people, Luedtke did something even more important. He helped us kids, both boys and girls, realize that what we were learning growing up on farms was important and would do us well as adults. We kids learned that working hard, getting along with others, showing up on time, and doing the best possible job were important no matter what your job or where you lived. Luedtke also helped us appreciate country life, neighbors, and taking time to watch a sunset. Those were the days when a considerable rift still existed between town kids and country kids. The idea that country kids could do anything besides farm was seen as impossible.

A few years after George and Ruth Luedtke moved to our neighborhood, they invited Ruth's parents, Mr. and Mrs. Walter Stroesser of Milwaukee, to live with them. Walter Stroesser was a little man with white hair, a thick white mustache, and a ruddy complexion; he used to run a tailor shop in downtown Milwaukee. If we thought the Luedtkes were a little strange, Walter Stroesser set a new standard for strangeness.

Politically speaking, our neighborhood consisted of mostly Republicans, a handful of Democrats, and a considerable number of people who voted for the person rather than the party. Then along comes Stroesser, a Socialist—a political party mostly, if not completely, unknown to folks in our neighborhood. Turns out Milwaukee had had a Socialist mayor for years, and Stroesser had been active in Milwaukee Socialist politics.

Walter Stroesser took a liking to the neighborhood kids, including me. When we stopped by the Luedtkes for one thing or another, I often talked to Mr. Stroesser, as we kids called him. He asked about country things, how we liked living on a farm—questions we struggled to answer because we'd never lived anywhere else. He asked us what we liked to read, which books, which authors. No one had ever asked me questions like that before. He asked how we liked school and said we should get as much schooling as possible and that we should keep on learning no matter what.

"There's always something new to learn," he said. Mr. Stroesser was a good example because he was always reading, always asking questions, always probing into this and that. I was so impressed that he listened to us kids, what we had to say, what we were thinking about. I never forgot that.

In one of those conversations, Mr. Stroesser asked me if I had heard of Carl Sandburg. I said I remembered reading about him in high school English class.

"Sandburg is one of my friends," Mr. Stroesser said softly. He brought out several of Sandburg's books—signed, first-edition copies—to show me.

I couldn't believe it. Here was a man who actually knew someone I had studied in school. Mr. Stroesser told me Sandburg had lived in Milwaukee for several years and, like Stroesser himself, was active in the Socialist Party, serving as socialist Mayor Emil Seidel's secretary from 1910 to 1912. I was dumbfounded. We had an important man living in our neighborhood who knew even more important men.

I suspect few people knew about Mr. Stroesser's impressive connections in the political and literary world. But they continued to judge him as strange, mostly because he walked around the block every day. Understand, a country block ran four miles, a mile on each side. Folks couldn't figure out why Mr. Stroesser would walk and not go anywhere. We all walked a lot, but not for the sake of walking. We walked to check on crops, to hunt, to visit the neighbors, or to follow a team of horses pulling a plow or a drag.

In our community, if you were out driving and saw someone walking, you stopped and offered the person a ride. Mr. Stroesser always refused. And not only did he refuse, he wouldn't even pass the time of day. He would point to his watch and keep on walking. "Crazy old bugger was timing himself," Bill Miller said once, after offering Mr. Stroesser a ride and being turned down.

The years passed, the Stroessers died, and the Luedtke boys grew up and left home. Eventually, George Luedtke took a job in Wautoma and he and Ruth moved out of our neighborhood. His farm mostly sat vacant. But George Luedtke and Walter Stroesser had become a part of our community. People had come to accept them for who they were. In his own strange way, Luedtke encouraged—and mostly succeeded—in having our quiet, mostly reserved rural community look at itself in a new, interesting way. And though most folks saw Walter Stroesser as an oddity, he showed me that curiosity and a love for good books opened doors, no matter where you lived or what you ended up doing. Through his words and actions, he also taught me it was okay to be a little different, to listen to another voice, to do things others did not.

Later, other city folks bought property in our neighborhood; some even tried to farm. But none had as much influence on the people as did George Luedtke or Walter Stroesser.

CHAPTER 27

~

A Farm Remembers

Television set—$200.00
Scholarship, University of Wisconsin—$63.50

A few years after electricity came to our neighborhood, television arrived. Pa was one of the first to buy a set, in 1951, when I was seventeen years old. The TV set was a huge piece of furniture with a tiny screen. He bought it from the Wild Rose Midland Cooperative store for two hundred dollars, which included the cost of installation and a complicated antenna that rose several feet from our roof and consisted of aluminum crossbars of various lengths that pointed in the direction of the nearest TV station— in Green Bay.

Soon, everyone had a television set. Television had a near hyp- notic appeal for both rural and town people. People who didn't have a telephone owned a TV. People who still milked cows by hand owned a TV. People who couldn't afford indoor plumbing owned a TV—true for my folks. Pa snapped on the big box after evening chores and left it on into the night. The little screen with its moving black-and-white pictures transfixed us.

Television altered our community activities dramatically; it even changed our sleep patterns. Ma and Pa stayed up to the watch the ten o'clock news; before, like most farm folks, they tucked themselves into bed by that time to rise at five the next morning. Now, our cows had to wait to be milked later in the morning, because Pa couldn't get up as early as he had before TV.

Neighborhood card parties and dances declined, as did community gatherings at the country schoolhouse. We all stayed home, glued to the glowing TV set. We watched the Ed Sullivan variety show on Sunday nights; Jack Benny and Red Skelton; the *Adventures of Ozzie and Harriet* and *I Love Lucy*; the *Honeymooners* with Art Carney and Jackie Gleason; the local and national news; and the weather.

Meantime, electricity made possible all sorts of practical technology—electric lights, radios, washing machines, irons, fans, refrigerators. Outside, electric motors pumped water, ran milking machines, powered tractors, elevated hay bales into haymows, bathed barns with light, unloaded silage from silos, and cleaned barns. All this technology resulted in less labor needed on the farm, even as farmers milked more cows and grew more acres of corn, oats, and alfalfa.

Young men and women began leaving the farm right after high school, at age eighteen, looking for work. They moved to cities like Madison, Racine, Kenosha, La Crosse, Milwaukee, Chicago, Minneapolis, and St. Paul. The men worked in auto plants, tanneries and paper mills, farm-implement factories, breweries, and heavy industry—doing manual labor, mostly. The women went off to be secretaries in these same businesses. In my community, about three-quarters of the young people of my generation left for the city. A handful went on to college. Many came home every weekend because they hated city life and detested their jobs. But they were caught. For most, there was no room on the farm, and few had skills to advance far in the companies where they worked. (When these same people reached retirement age, many moved back to the country, to the same community they had left thirty or more years earlier. It was not their choice to live in the city. In retirement, they finally had a choice.)

In the 1950s, student numbers began dropping at country schools across the Midwest. Folks began talking about closing the Chain O' Lake School my brothers and I—and our mother before us—had attended. Educational researchers from the University of Wisconsin in Madison said the remaining children in our neighborhood would obtain a better education at a consolidated school in Wild Rose. They offered research and test-score results from consolidated schools across the Midwest to make their case.

After the 1954–1955 term, the school board closed the one-room country schoolhouse and sold it to the community for one dollar. The community tried to keep up the building as a community center, but no one had money for maintenance or electric bills. The schoolhouse never had indoor plumbing, but an electric motor powered the water pump in the pump house, and the building had electric lights. In a couple years, the community sold the school to a former neighbor boy and his wife for a summer home. He had moved to Chicago many years earlier. For most of the year, grass and weeds grew tall and the teeter-totter stood unused; in winter, the snow piled high on the front steps. Eventually, the well-worn base paths of the softball diamond returned to grass, the many games played there now only a memory.

What the research did not show was the importance of the school to our community, beyond the education it provided the children. The country school gave our community an identity, the same way a post office identifies a town. Ask someone in our neighborhood where they lived and they told you Chain O' Lake, the name of our school.

The schoolhouse was also the center of social activities, the place to celebrate birthdays and anniversaries, the place to hold card parties and dances, and the place where I was welcomed home in 1954 when I returned from a stint in the army. This was the last time I visited the building while it still operated as a school.

I doubt many people realized how important the country school was to them until it closed and their children climbed on shiny school buses and rode to the town school.

The story of the home farm wouldn't be complete without saying what happened to Pa and Ma, to my brothers and me, and to the home farm. For me, one late April day, the principal of Wild Rose High School called me into his office. You always feared the worst when this happened. But Mr. Ruzicka told me I was valedictorian of my class and would be awarded a scholarship for one semester's tuition to attend the University of Wisconsin in Madison. This news came as a surprise. I had always liked school and knew I was doing reasonably well, especially in English and the math and science courses. But I didn't realize I was the top person in my class. I'd just never considered that.

Suddenly I was confronted with one of the most difficult tasks in my life: informing Pa that I had a chance to go to college. I knew, as the oldest son, that he expected me to stay home and farm after high school. I truly liked farming, still do, so staying would not have been difficult for me. But now I faced accepting or turning down a scholarship to a school a hundred miles from home.

Neither Pa nor Ma had graduated from eighth grade, so the notion of my brothers or me going to college was a new, little-thought-about possibility. I once heard my Uncle Fred, Pa's brother, say, "The only reason anybody goes to college is to get out of work." I don't remember Pa answering Uncle Fred's pronouncement.

When I returned home from school that night, I went out to the barn, where Pa was doing chores. "Pa," I said hesitantly. "I've got some news." He stopped forking straw and looked at me.

"I talked to the principal today," I said. "He told me they have a semester's scholarship for me to attend the University of

Wisconsin in Madison. He said I had to let him know in a day or so whether I would accept it."

For what seemed like an eternity, Pa didn't say anything. "You want to go to college?" he finally asked.

"I don't know," I answered.

"How much is the scholarship worth?" Pa asked.

"$63.50."

Again, Pa said nothing. He fluffed-up some straw he was spreading behind the cows.

"That's a pretty good hunk of money. Shame to let it go to waste. Better accept it."

"I've been thinking of enrolling in the College of Agriculture," I said. "Mr. Millar, the ag teacher, told me about it."

"Good idea. You might learn something we can use here on the farm." A grin tried to spread across Pa's face, but he was having trouble with it. I think he knew that once I went off to college, the chances of my coming back to farm were not good.

He was right. I won additional scholarships and stayed on to earn a bachelor's degree in agricultural education. After college, instead of returning to the home farm, I spent some time in the army, out east. When I came back to the Midwest, I applied for a research assistantship at the university and earned a master of science degree, again in agriculture. Upon completion, I took a job as a county extension agent, like Henry Haferbecker had been, first in Green Lake County and later in Brown County—both in Wisconsin. Then I worked for a few years as a publication editor for the Wisconsin State 4-H office. Eventually, I returned to UW–Madison and earned a PhD. I spent the next thirty years as a professor of agriculture at the University of Wisconsin–Madison before taking early retirement to write full time.

My brothers left the home farm as well. Darrel earned a PhD and went on to teach at the University of Kentucky and at Pennsylvania State University, and he served as an administrator at a prestigious garden in Pennsylvania. He eventually settled in New Jersey, where he owned a greenhouse and nursery and has a national reputation for developing prize-winning daylilies. He has since moved back to Wild Rose, where he continues to develop new daylilies on a more limited basis. His twin brother, Donald, stayed closer to home, spending a year farming with Pa, then leaving for barber college. For many years, he owned a five-chair barber/style shop in Sheboygan, a hundred miles east of Wild Rose; he now owns a barbershop in Neshkoro, just twenty miles south of the farm where we grew up.

Even though we all three left the farm, it profoundly influenced each of us. Each of us, I'm sure without being fully aware of it happening, developed a deep love for the land and the world of nature, and an unwavering respect for the small family farm where parents and kids worked together, played together, experienced joy and sorrow, and grew up stronger because of it.

And all three of us married farm girls. My wife, Ruth, and I have owned a small farm just west of Wild Rose since 1966. We grow a large garden, do prairie restoration, and grow pine trees; I do much of my writing there. Donald and his wife, Marcie, live on thirty-three acres they own next to my farm, where they garden, plant wildlife crops, and enjoy the out-of-doors.

With all three boys gone, Pa continued to milk cows, and Ma continued to take care of the chickens, her garden, and her strawberry patch. There were no more acres of cucumbers and green beans. When Donald left, the last son to do so, Pa bought a new barn cleaner, a mechanical device powered by an electric motor that automatically cleaned the gutters behind the cows and deposited the manure directly in a manure spreader.

In March 1964, Pa held an auction and sold his cows. I traveled home from my teaching job in Madison to help. This was clearly Pa's second-saddest day on the farm, exceeded only by the day the cattle trucks shipped our herd of brucellosis-infected cattle off to slaughter.

That March afternoon, when the auctioneer banged his gavel for the last time, cattle trucks once more backed up to the barn and the cows were loaded. Tears welled in Pa's eyes as, together, we stood at the barn door watching the last truck leave. The once warm and friendly barn now stood cold and quiet. No rustling of cattle in their stanchions, no calves blatting for their evening milk, no barn cats gathering at their milk pans. Just the faint smell of alfalfa, corn silage, and cow manure. An era had passed. As it turned out, this barn would never house dairy cattle again.

For most of the next ten years, Pa kept several beef cattle in the barn. He took care of them, grew several acres of corn, and made hay. He took over some of Ma's duties in the garden and strawberry patch, though she kept sole control of her chickens. During those years, Pa also did more fishing than when he milked cows twice a day.

Pa would have liked to live out his life on the farm, but Ma had always wanted to live in the village of Wild Rose. She grew up during a time when successful farmers turned their farms over to their children and moved to town to enjoy their last years. In May 1973, they sold the farm and moved to Wild Rose, population about seven hundred fifty, but way too big a place for Pa, who preferred the peace and quiet of the country.

With the farm sold to a non-farmer, the new owner soon divided up the one hundred sixty acres. Most recently, six families lived on the land. A Christmas-tree company owns about forty acres; beautiful evergreens now grow where we planted corn and alfalfa.

Something similar happened to the rest of the farms in the neighborhood. Much of the land has been divided. All the owners work off the farm, some traveling forty miles to Stevens Point or sixty miles to Appleton for work. No one milks cows. The barns that haven't fallen down stand empty or are used for storage.

Both Pa and Ma died in 1993. Pa was ninety-three and Ma ninety-one. They rest now only a few miles from the farm that meant so much to them and made such a difference in the lives of their three sons. The land remains, as do the memories and the stories. The home farm had a story to tell; every farm has a story to tell. Pa and Ma lived for nearly fifty years on this farm; it was so much a part of their lives, as it was a part of the lives of their three boys who grew up there.

As Ma and Pa prepared to move off the home farm, they held a second auction. My brother Donald and I returned home to help. The day of the auction—May 5, 1973—neighbors and strangers came to bid on Pa's old machinery, Ma's extra household goods, and the remaining stock of straw, corn, and hay. Pa watched dry-eyed as his fellow farmers bid on his old Farmall H and C tractors, his 1950 Chevrolet pickup, a corn and a grain binder, and assorted other equipment. He had an easier time with this auction than when he sold the cows. Cows were special for Pa, and he sometimes let slip that he preferred driving horses to driving tractors.

I suspect this second auction affected me more than Pa. I knew this would be my last day on the home farm. After today, I could no longer call it home. As I reviewed the auction bill, each piece of equipment brought back memories. The pitchforks reminded me of bunching loose hay during the hot days of early July. The "75 ft. 8-inch endless belt" was the one that connected our tractor to the threshing machine, and the pleasant memories of threshing season returned. The "two-section spring tooth harrow" reminded me of the many days I drove a team pulling this harrow, walking behind in a cloud of dirty yellow dust. The "New Idea manure spreader" brought back the memory of shoveling manure and hauling it to a back field where we spread it, on a cold spring day or an even colder winter day. The chicken feeders and brooder returned me to when Ma took care of the chickens, from the time they were peeping chicks until they were mature layers. "Monitor hit and miss fly wheel engine and pump jack, runs good"—oh, what memories that old gasoline engine brought back, of pumping water in the years before electricity came to our farm.

I saw all the artifacts of my growing-up years one more time and recalled the stories, smells, sounds, and feelings that went along with each item. It was like a funeral visitation, where you deal with your emotions and memories, give your respects, and say your goodbyes.

About the Author

Author Jerry Apps was born and raised on a central-Wisconsin dairy farm in the days before electricity or indoor plumbing. His family farmed used kerosene lanterns, gasoline engines, a team of draft horses, and a homemade tractor converted from a truck. During Jerry's growing-up years, he witnessed the second great revolution in farming—the arrival of electric lines to rural areas, running water in barns, and new farm machines like tractors, balers, and combines.

A professor emeritus of agriculture at the University of Wisconsin–Madison, Jerry has written more than forty fiction, nonfiction, and children's books, many of them on rural history and country life. Recent books include *The Quiet Season: Remembering Country Winters*, *Whispers and Shadows: A Naturalist's Memoir*, *Never Curse the Rain: A Farm Boy's Reflections on Water*, and *Old Farm County Cookbook* (with his daughter, Susan Apps-Bodilly).

Jerry's writing has won awards from the American Library Association, the Wisconsin Library Association, the Wisconsin Historical Society, and the Council for Wisconsin Writers, among others. He has created four documentaries about farm life and country living with Wisconsin Public Television. Jerry and his wife, Ruth, have three children, seven grandchildren, and two great-grandsons. They divide their time between their home in Madison and their farm, Roshara, near Wild Rose, Wisconsin.